A Journey To Self Love

Memoirs of a Butterfly

Armetria M. Charles

A Journey to Self Love © 2009 by Armetria M. Charles

All rights reserved. Except as permitted under the U.S. Copyright Act of 1976, no part of this publication may be reproduced, distributed, or transmitted in any form or by any means, or stored in a database or retrieval system, without the prior written permission of the publisher.

If you have purchased this book with a "dull" or "missing" cover, you may have purchased an unauthorized or stolen book. Please immediately contact the publisher advising where, when, and how you purchased the book.

Editing and Typesetting: Carla M. Dean, U Can Mark My Word

Printed in the United States of America

First Edition

ISBN#: 978-0-557-54479-0

Published by:

Armetria Speaks,
1380 Monroe Street NW #200
Washington, DC 20002

Visit the website at: www.armetriamcharles.com
Email: armetriaspeaks@gmail.com

This Book Is Affectionately Dedicated To:

My beloved husband, Frederick A Charles;
My wonderful, supportive father, Varis L. Knight;
And my awesome children,
Andre, Isaiah, Kametri, Jeremiah, and Nicholas.

In Loving Memory Of:

My beloved older brother, Michael Lawrence Harrison.

You will never be forgotten.

TABLE OF CONTENTS

Acknowledgements	9
A Letter to My Readers	11
Introduction	13
Ch. 1 – Beauty Is In the Eye of the Beholder	17
Ch. 2 – Rejecting the Abandonment	23
Ch. 3 – The Fear Trap	41
Ch. 4 – Counterfeit Love	55
Ch. 5 – The Keys to Accepting Me	65
Ch. 6 – The Fast Break from Self Pity	75
Ch. 7 – Forgiveness: The Bitter Struggle	81
Ch. 8 – The Tug of War in Forgiving Me	95
Ch. 9 – Picking up the Pieces	111
Ch. 10 – The WOW Factor	119
About the Author	123

Acknowledgements

Though it is virtually impossible for me to list all those who have influenced me and contributed to make this book a reality, I will recognize a special few.

To my husband, **Frederick A. Charles**, the love of my life, I wish to express my deepest appreciation for your constant love, support, encouragement, and belief in me.

To my beloved father, **Varis Knight**, I am humbly grateful to you for being supportive and instrumental in making me the lady I am today. Thank you for teaching me "how to go through the valley to get to the mountain".

To my sweet **Nana**, you are the one who gave me shelter and showed me what a home was when no one else would have me. You showed me the meaning of independence and taught me how to be a loving mother. Through your influence, I learned how to not rely on the welfare system and create my own future. Words can never express my love, gratitude, and appreciation.

To **Aunt D.**, you have been a shining example of a loving, supportive wife and mother. And exemplifying the beauty of a woman is internal.

To **Aunt M.**, I am grateful for your tough love and go-getter attitude. I thank God for using you to talk my mother out of aborting me. Without you, there would be no "Meatball".

To **Pastor Jonathan Carson, thanks** for your wisdom, prayers, and guidance, and also thanks to **First Lady Marjorie Carson** for your shining example of what a Godly woman is to be.

To **Stacy Williams** for displaying selfless acts of kindness and for standing in the gap as a mother for me.

To my special friends for their prayers, love, and support throughout this process: **Reshma Block, Terrinda S. Davidson, Shelby & British Hill, Regina Hollins, Michelle Jackson, and Nicole Waddell.**

To the many who have poured into my life in immeasurable ways, I am grateful.

A Letter to My Readers

Beloved,

I would like to take a moment to personally thank you and welcome you to *A Journey to Self Love: Memoirs of a Butterfly*.

In this book, you will find a lot of traumatic, tumultuous events that imprint my past and charted the course of my destiny.

I want to let it be known, I love each and every person mentioned in this book. They have affected my life, whether in the positive or in the negative. They have all been used for God's glory, according to Romans 8:28.

In no way, shape, or form is this book intended to exploit my loved ones. Yet, this is a work that I have published to exploit the enemy.

The Bible says we all have fallen short of the glory of God. So, at this time, I pray that the eyes of your understanding are opened and all eyes of judgment are closed.

When writing this piece, I wrote from the perspective of how I interpreted the events as they took place – as a child.

I pray none of my family members are offended and that they see the great good of being used in a story of deliverance and triumph.

I thank God for you and for your continued support. May you be abundantly blessed by this publication.

Lovingly,
Armetria

Introduction

A butterfly undergoes many changes before it can be considered a beautiful work of art, carefully crafted in the hands of a loving father. Allow me to share with you a quick story of metamorphosis in my own words. This will help you to understand my struggles, triumphs, passion, and pain, as it was very necessary during my personal metamorphosis.

A mother butterfly drops an egg from the sky whereby the soon-to-be butterfly is first abandoned by its mother. It hatches to become a peculiar little creature first referred to as a caterpillar or larva. The caterpillar or larva stage is a very vital stage in the life cycle of a butterfly.

The caterpillar fights to absorb large quantities of food to ensure proper growth in which it's very vulnerable to its predators. It spends a lot of time and energy in its struggle for growth and life. It goes through four changes of skin to accommodate the large food quantities it must take in. During this process, the larva is in grave danger and must survive for two months bypassing predators whose mission is to devour it. It must carefully crawl to a tree, while trying not to be stepped on, picked up, and entrapped by humans, or eaten by birds and other flying creatures. It must be driven enough to want to live and must find the value in the change.

It must not allow any of life's circumstances to stop it from getting to its destination, the tree. During its pursuit of climbing the tree, it is not out of harm's way. Although the vulnerable larva is often well camouflaged, it does not guarantee its survival, as there are creatures lurking and waiting to make a meal out of it. There also may be tree sap that traps the larva, thus slowing it down or causing a long, slow death by enslaving it.

After all of that, the determined creature makes it to a safe place on the tree. It begins the process of undergoing changes that will one day make it one of the most beautiful insects you have ever laid eyes on.

The first stage is called the pupa, which I like to call the transformation. It is one of nature's greatest wonders; how can an active larva become a pupa with no ability to move? Although it seems to be stuck and stagnate in life, the God of all creation is taking it through some dynamite changes that are not visible to the larva or us.

Interestingly, there is one more change in which the skin splits to reveal a wet, glistering creature that appears to still be a caterpillar hunched up. This is a perfect illustration that God does not lead us blindfolded throughout the journey; He will give us a peek into our greatness to come. Before the final transformation of the final stage, the creature fastens itself in its silk while the metamorphosis is completed.

With the metamorphosis completed, the adult butterfly breaks the pupal case, pulls itself out, and hangs upside-down with its wings wet and limp. Proudly, it begins immediately expanding its wings and flapping as it calls forth blood flow and life into the veins of the wings. Once the wings are dry and strong, the butterfly is ready to take flight for the first time. The freshly emerged beautiful butterfly will fly to seek nourishment and then seek a perfect mate, thus creating new beauty in the world. To fulfill this task, the butterfly will have to brave the weathers, the unsettled environment conditions, and of course, it has to always be wary of predators. After all of the wonderful, painstaking changes this magnificent creature had to undergo, its beauty will only last for one summer.

Allow me to invite you on a journey where you get to experience a true metamorphosis through the eyes of yours truly, Armetria M. Charles.

A JOURNEY TO SELF LOVE

BEAUTY IS IN THE EYE OF THE BEHOLDER

Chapter 1

ARMETRIA M. CHARLES

Beauty Is In the Eye of the Beholder

The journey for me began when I finally decided I wasn't going to be hurt anymore. I had erected many walls around myself that harbored shame, failure, and defeat, until I literally hated myself and all that I stood for at a very young, tender age. As a result of the verbal abuse I suffered from my maternal grandmother, I felt like I didn't have a snowball's chance in hell of ever thinking I was beautiful. Although people would tell me that I was a pretty girl, I never believed them. I would always find a way to brush the compliments off with a phony smile or by rolling my eyes in the back of my head in disbelief. I would hear the questions and thoughts echoing in my head. *Who? Me? Pretty? Yeah, right! Are they referring to my looks? They're just saying that to have something nice to say.* I had every reason why I believed people were lying to me. I sure didn't feel beautiful, let alone look it.

My mother was absolutely beautiful! She was young, tall, had straight hair, green eyes, and was "light skinned!" You are probably asking yourself, why on earth is being light skinned the highlight of my mother's beauty? Well, let me think...perhaps it came from having a grandmother who was very vocal about her opinions that lighter complexions and fine textured hair were the epitome of beauty. You have probably figured out that I was not her cup of tea, especially in the looks department. She simply could not accept the fact that I was a little browner than she expected with hair that fought against me like two drunks fighting in front of a liquor store just before closing. I had learned to accept that darker skin tone wasn't a pretty image and nappy hair was even worse.

Getting back to the reason I simply didn't believe I was ever beautiful enough for anything or anyone. With those self-hatred spirits instilled in me at such a young age, I grew up relying on all kinds of products, skin bleach creams, and hair weaves to try and reinvent a more beautiful me. Seems no matter how hard I tried, at the end of the day, the makeup would be washed off, the weave would eventually wear out, and I would be stuck with the original old me. I had learned to hate myself and believed that I was ugly. I felt I was not pretty enough to ever consider being anything close to the Barbie dolls I liked to play with. As a matter of fact, I didn't have any black dolls. I was simply taught that who I was and how I looked was not considered beautiful.

Often, my mother and grandmother would make reference to when I was born. My mother would say, "You were so ugly and black, I began to cry that this can't be my baby." Then she said my grandmother looked over at her and said, "Well, look at the tools you used to make her." If you haven't figured it out already, my beloved father is beautifully dark-skinned.

Reflections

Perhaps you noticed in this chapter that I had ignorantly adopted my grandmother's perception on what beauty was defined as: light-skinned and straight hair. Later on in life, I discovered these were not the defining factors of beauty. Yet, beauty is a number of characteristics that starts on the inside and radiates outwardly. Beauty is present in all shapes, sizes, colors, and even hair textures. As a matter of fact, some of the most beautiful people I have ever encountered in life weren't ones that you'd typically find on the cover of beauty myopic magazines.

Healing Balm for the Soul

You have the power of choice in a belittling situation or environment. You possess the power to reject or receive the poisoning beliefs, words, and actions of others. The first step in loving yourself and accepting the real authentic you is being very clear and comfortable in saying this phrase: "I don't receive that." This is applicable when it's someone else imposing their ideologies on you or even your own inner voice of terror. Take those thoughts captive.

"...For the weapons of our warfare are not physical [weapons of flesh and blood], but they are mighty before God for the overthrow and destruction of strongholds, [Inasmuch as we] refute arguments and theories and reasonings and every proud and lofty thing that sets itself up against the [true] knowledge of God; and we lead every thought and purpose away captive into the obedience of Christ (the Messiah, the Anointed One)..."

2 Corinthians 10: 4-5

So, the next time you are inundated with other people's perceptions of your beauty and even your own inner voice of terror, simply respond with "I don't receive that."

"The Lord does not look at the things man looks at. Man looks at the outward appearance, but the Lord looks at the heart."

1 Samuel 16:7 (New International Version)

"Charm is deceptive and beauty is fleeting, but a woman who fears the Lord is to be praised."

Proverbs 31:30 (New International Version)

"I praise You because I am fearfully and wonderfully made; Your works are wonderful, I know that full well."

Psalm 139:14 (New International Version)

Now whose report should I believe…God's or my grandmother's? Whose report should you believe…God's or the enemy's?

How does it feel to hear what the Word of God has to say in reference to you and your beauty? How does it feel to know you are fearfully and wonderfully made?

A Love Letter to You

Beloved,

Doesn't it feel awesome to get clarity and discover there's no evidence to support that you are unattractive for whatever physical reason? God has sent me to tell you that no matter the physical appearance "there could never be a more beautiful you." Now, go love yourself. You are one of God's greatest creations, fearfully and wonderfully made. When He made you, He said, "Marvelous are thy works." When He was done creating you, He said, "It was all good." (Genesis 1:31)

Lovingly,
Armetria

A JOURNEY TO SELF LOVE

REJECTING THE ABANDONMENT

Chapter 2

ARMETRIA M. CHARLES

Rejecting the Abandonment

One of the hardest things for me to come to grips with was being rejected. Wanting love from my mother — rejected! Needing love from my father — rejected! Love from the family as a whole — rejected! I never felt there could be a perfect, loving family anywhere in the world for me.

However, I soon discovered that family played a very serious role in preparing me for the world as I'd known it. Even after moving in with my paternal grandmother, whom I knew loved me and did the very best she could to care for me, I suffered rejection. I wasn't a perfect child, and having already gone through so much hurt and pain, I acted out and misbehaved. No one could seem to understand that I had some serious issues, and being what folks considered normal was an uphill struggle for me.

In my rejected eyes, my grandmother acted as a protector for my father, but I had no clue what she was trying to protect him from. Me? I would ask him for small amounts of money, a dollar or so, and it seemed that my father was always happy to give it to me. However, if my grandmother were around, she would intercept and say, "What you need a dollar for?"

I would reply, "To get something from the store." Sometimes the expression on her face would reveal a look of pain, as if it literally pained her to see my father give me something. Perhaps since I was broken upon my arrival with Nana, I viewed her lessons of saving money as more rejection.

I would play games at the carnival and do other things that children do, and it seemed that I would never win. I always thought of myself as an absolute loser, a reject of the blessings that anyone else would receive. I seemed to always fall under the radar of my peer's perfection. Everyone else seemed to have parents in their lives…if not both, then at least one.

My dad had this friend named Tim, and Tim had a daughter who achieved straight A's in school. My dad would always compare me to her and wonder why I couldn't make good grades, as well. As far as I knew, I was not very smart. It was hard for me to concentrate in school with all of the abuse I had been through. Besides, being compared to her caused me to suffer with rejection and low self-esteem all the more because I didn't know how to be like her. I only knew how to be the broken fragmented pieces of me.

While living with my maternal grandmother, I felt rejection all of the time. She was famous for making me feel left out. I had to share a room with my older uncle, her youngest son. He was a spoiled brat; everything he wanted he was given. Of course, he had become angry because he had to share his room with me.

I could always feel the difference in the love my grandmother had for the both of us. For instance, when she would make meals for my siblings and me, we would have something like a salad, ravioli, dessert, and a beverage. Personally, I felt that was great! My grandmother did what she could to feed us, and it was always a three-course meal…even if it was once in a can. However, my uncle's meals were always something that sent a salivating aroma throughout the entire apartment. Perhaps it would be the savory smell of a delicious quarter pounder with cheese, French fries, or whatever else he wanted. I wanted that, also, but when I would ask, I was fussed at terribly and reminded of how bad my life was.

My grandmother would say, "His father sends money to buy him that food. Your father is in jail. You don't have a father. You get on my (curse word) nerves with always wanting his stuff. This is his house! You don't even belong here. You belong to your mother and your father, and they don't even want you!"

I never felt like I belonged and was incredibly damaged.

Sometimes my uncle would have fits of rage and flick off for no reason, throwing TV's and whatever else his hands could find to toss. Many times he would fight me, as well. One day, he decided to repeat what he heard his mom say about my dad. That's when I tried to fight him back, which resulted in him tossing me and busting the back of my head.

Upset, my grandmother tended to my needs, but her mouth would always convey how she really felt about me. "You could have killed her and gone to jail making her hit her head like that, and you have no right upsetting him like that. This is his house and that is his room. You don't belong here! I will be glad when your mother comes and gets you."

She and I both knew my mother was never coming to get me. I was a total reject and she knew it.

My mother would visit us every three to five months, and that was mostly to eat and sleep, not to see me. During her stay, my grandmother would use her to chastise us and do our hair. Once my mother was rested, clean, and fed, she was gone again. There were no phone calls or any other type of contact in between her visits. I don't know how that made my sister feel, but I felt unworthy of any affection. Can you blame me for feeling that way when I wasn't even worth a phone call from my birth mother?

I use to love lying up under my mother when she came to visit. I loved to suck my thumb, while playing with her ears and elbows. Doing that was comforting to me. However, she would say, "Stop, you little freak!" I wasn't a freak, though. I was just seeking comfort and security from her. Perhaps because she didn't come around very often, she didn't know who I was and what my needs were. So, I received the rejection and simply lay there playing with my own elbow or ear.

Once I moved in with my nana and dad, which was something I always wanted, my dad moved out. I felt abandoned immediately. He soon got a beautiful home that he shared with his significant other. I visited and even spent the night a couple times, but what I wanted was to live with him. I thought by enduring the struggle with living with my maternal grandmother that I would be rewarded residence with my father. I was broken! Once I was released to be with him and make up for the many years we missed together, he moved out for someone he felt was more important than I.

I felt I simply didn't matter! I asked him if I could live with him in his beautiful home, and of course, I was rejected. He said, "I don't think it would be fair to allow you to stay here." Perhaps he had a good reason, but to a child, it sounded like he was living the life and I was not invited. Every time I would watch him get into one of his elaborate vehicles, whether the drop top Mercedes Benz or the Range Rover, and drive away, I felt abandoned and rejected. I don't think he ever understood nor did I think he even cared about how I felt.

Nana and my father had come from the era that children were to be seen and not heard. It backfired because one way or another I would be heard!

I had so many abandonment issues that it played a major part in causing any peace in my life to be disrupted. I was moved from household to household. I went from being with my mom, to my maternal grandmother, to my paternal grandmother, to my father's girlfriend, to a friend of the family's house, back to my paternal grandmother, to a McDonald's co-worker's home, to my boyfriend and his mom's, to a girlfriend and her mother's home, to one of my dad's friend's home, to another girlfriend's home, back to my boyfriend and his mother's, and to the next-door neighbor's home of my friend. It was rough. I was basically homeless.

Choosing to be a victim to the spirit of abandonment and rejection caused a great deal of defeat in my life. I displayed it through my actions. I would end a relationship with someone before it could really begin. I had some awesome people in my life that were there to truly add to the quality of it. However, I treated those people horribly. I would gossip about them, become jealous of them, backbite, slander, and destroy.

I never knew why relationships would always come to an abrupt end in my life. I simply thought I was always right. Someone was always out to get me, trying to figure out how to get rid of me, or talking about me. So, I would test them until they left. Or I would release them first, whether it would be to just let the relationship go with nothing else said or to destroy it with some of the destructive tools mentioned above.

When I got a divorce in my first marriage, it was a form of rejection, although I wanted very badly to be separated from all of the mental abuse I suffered while in the union. There was a ripping in my spirit that I couldn't explain and still can't explain. It was painful and refreshing all at the same time. I was severely offended in my spirit walking in rejection and never knew it until now.

I remember when I was pregnant with my first son and my aunt's sister-in-law was in the hospital dying of cancer. I think my grandmother told me that her sister-in-law wanted to see me. My grandmother made it very clear that she had higher hopes for me. Therefore, she did not want me to disclose to her that I was pregnant because the news might make her more ill and cause her to pass along faster. I decided not to go see her or call because that was a form of rejection to me, as well. My feelings were very hurt, but as usual, I packed them away and kept it moving.

When it was time to have my first baby, I was very afraid because I was suffering with toxemia. My blood pressure was through the roof, and I was petrified that I was going to lose my life. I had already started to lose my eyesight due to my high blood pressure. The polite nurse had even brought me some paperwork on leaving a will.

"I'm only eighteen and have nothing. What will I leave?" I told her, then cried thinking about it.

I called my nana looking for my dad to come and support me in the birth of my new baby boy. Although my dad had his hang-ups, if I called on him, he would be right there. My nana (my father's protector) told me that my father wasn't there and that she hadn't spoken with him yet. However, I felt that was not the truth since she normally spoke with my father everyday and sometimes even twice a day. When I asked her if she would come to visit me, she replied, "I don't go to hospitals when people have babies."

I remember crying because my child's father's entire family was there shaking their heads and talking about how it was a shame that none of my family was there for support. I finally got a hold of my dad who lit up my world when he walked through the door. I love him so much. I remember thinking it didn't matter who showed up after that because my knight was now there!

He came in with all sorts of gifts and goodies for the baby and me. I was so thrilled. After he left, they still talked trash about how I had no support, though. When my auntie called, she didn't sound enthusiastic at all about the birth of my child. She simply asked, "Why you wanna breastfeed?" My paternal grandmother always says a baby is nothing to get excited over. I harbored all of that rejection I felt from my family not being there for me in my heart. I was a wounded woman with a heart filled with pain.

I experienced much segregation in my family, while it seemed like my cousins always received "cream of the crop" treatment. I now have five beautiful boys and I love them dearly. We were invited to visit the family at my aunt's home and we had an awesome time. My uncle, aunt, and cousin were visiting from Mississippi, and the entire family gathered to celebrate. Later that day, my little cousin from Mississippi had asked me if I was going to be coming to the dinner the next day at my father's youngest sister's home. I said, "Oh, I suppose. I knew nothing about it."

"Yeah, the whole family is coming, so you are invited, too," she replied.

I thought about it and realized that if I were invited, I would have known about the dinner just like everyone else.

As I was leaving the celebration a while later, my dad approached me and asked, "Am I going to see you tomorrow at your aunt's?"

I explained to him, "Cousin just told me, but no one else told me about it. I'm not sure if I should come."

My dad said, "See you tomorrow." In other words, he was saying, "You can come."

Early the next day, I woke my husband and children up so we could get dressed. Then I called my nana to ask her what time we should appear at my aunt's. She sounded shocked that I knew they were having an event and began to stutter about how she knew nothing about it. Then I explained to her how I knew and that my dad even asked me about coming.

She said, "Oh…well, I guess you can come. Call and ask your aunt. I'm not even going, baby. Actually, I believe your aunt was only having that for the guests. Everyone is not invited."

I replied with such hurt feelings of rejection. "Oh, that's fine, Nana. I understand. I will stay home. Talk to you later."

I broke the news to my family. I knew my nana was going to be attending and so was the rest of the family. Only "my" immediate family was excluded. I never understood why.

I felt such rejection that it made me separate myself from my family because I was just tired of being the outcast. Every time I shared something I wanted or aspired to do or be, I was looked at sideways as if doing great things were impossible through me. As I shared ideas and dreams, death would be spoken by supposed loved ones before the egg of the dream could even be hatched. So, I learned to keep my dreams and visions locked away in the safety of my brokenness.

One of the most memorable places of rejection was when my school placed me on medication without my parent's permission. My dad and grandmother knew nothing about it. I was attending a school that gave juvenile delinquents another chance to step into their educational greatness. Overall it was a great school, but the staff did some things that were not in the best interest of me or other students.

I was in twelfth grade and doing pretty well in school. I was an average B-C student, but that wasn't good enough. It was a pilot school that had much to prove in order to get more resources and money to keep it going. They took me to see a shrink who felt I was depressed and needed anti-depressants. I expressed to the principal and the counselor that I didn't want to take medication. I didn't feel I needed it, but they threatened to toss me out of the school if I didn't take it. They also told me that I was not to share the information with my parent(s)/guardian(s).

I was called into the counselor's office everyday to be watched as I was forced to take this medication. I was afraid to tell my dad because the school told me I would be thrown out if I started a ruckus. My dad's girlfriend at the time helped me get into the school, so I felt the need to do what I was told to save face for her reputation.

The medicine made me feel awful. I explained this over and over to the school, but they felt I was just making up an excuse to get out of taking it. One Saturday morning, my grandmother noticed I had not left my room for the entire morning. I was going through some serious changes, as I was having an allergic reaction to the medication that I was secretly taking. I was stuttering and my eyes were dilating. My body was undergoing many changes. My play mom, who was the girlfriend of my dad, came into my room to check on me and noticed what was happening. She grabbed me to go outside so I could explain what was happening to my dad.

My father was never willing to listen to what she had to say in regards to the school. I suppose his reason was out of fear of being found out by the girlfriend that had helped me get into it. My dad and play mom were fussing back and forth in regards to my illness, and then I heard my father say he didn't have time for this. He drove away, and I really felt rejected after that. I felt my dad didn't care about what happened to me. Once again, my school got away with experimenting on me.

Later, my father notified the school, and I did not have to take it any longer since it made me ill. Afterwards, all hell broke loose. The school felt they had my dad in their pocket because his girlfriend was a great friend and a donor to the school. My dad always played it safe with them so the word wouldn't get out about my play mom, his other girlfriend. I loved my play mom. She would advocate for me because she saw the wrong, but she was quickly restricted from having any affiliation with my school. So then, I had no advocate.

It was time to start filling out college applications and begin taking the SAT's. I was most excited about putting my best foot forward and attending a college. One day, the school counselor went around the classroom with a piece of paper telling students to sign it while quickly counseling us.

I asked, "What am I signing?"

She responded, "Oh, this is just a quick form to sign that will give you extra time on the SAT's."

I replied, "Oh, okay. Thanks!"

She moved on to other students and got them to do the same. I thought nothing of it until I went one Saturday morning all ready to take my SAT's and realized my SAT slip was a different color than all of the other students testing.

The woman placing us in the classrooms to be tested looked at my form and said, "Why is your form pink? I have never seen one of these. You stand over here."

"I think I can explain," I replied. "My principal paid for the students in our school to have extra time."

She retorted, "Like I said, I never seen anything like this, and you can't pay for more time. Are you slow or special ED or something?"

I said, "No, of course not. He just paid for us to have more time."

As I stood there, the other students were ushered in to begin testing. All of the other students from my school elected to go in the school van to a testing center in Virginia. I chose Howard University's testing site because it was closer to my home and I could walk.

I stood there waiting and growing anxious. The lady had just asked me if I was slow or in Special Education. Finally, she came out and said, "Honestly, I don't know where you go because this is a testing center for kids who take normal SAT's."

I ran out of that place with my heart beating fast and my blood pumping through my body like an overheated locomotive. I cried and cried while walking blocks home in pure shame and embarrassment. Any bit of confidence I had was stripped from me at that very moment. I thought to myself maybe that woman didn't know what she was talking about. My school had told me they paid for extra time for me to take that test.

When I got home, my aunt, the youngest sister of my father, was there and asked me how my testing went. I explained to her everything that happened. I told her the lady was illiterate and couldn't seem to understand that my principal had paid for me to have extra time on the test. My aunt, who is also an educator, said to me, "Armetria, calm down. You cannot buy extra time for an SAT."

I said, "But that's what they said, Auntie."

She replied, "Trust me. I know the only way you could get extra time for SAT testing is if you have a disability of some sort." As I began to cry harder, she asked, "Were you ever diagnosed with some sort of disorder or illness that would affect the way you comprehend?"

I responded by saying, "No, not that I can think of."

She asked to see my SAT registration form. After reading it, she pointed and said, "See, right here it says that you are ADD."

"What is ADD?" I asked.

She explained it and I cried even more. "Auntie, would you come up to my school and talk to them? I have no clue why this could be."

She said, "Sure, with your dad's permission."

We asked my father, and because he totally trusted my aunt, he agreed. She came to the school, and they were shocked to see this little inner-city girl had an aunt who knew her stuff. They gave my aunt the runaround, trying to discourage her and make her leave. She would not back down, though. She pressed all the more for them to give her the name of some test that would disclose whether or not I was indeed ADD. When the principal came out and tried explaining, my aunt expressed her appreciation but was very adamant about getting the test results she requested hours ago. My school counselor came out with the saddest face ever and looked at me like I was some sort of plague. My aunt looked over the testing results and discovered there was no diagnosis for ADD. It simply said I had traits of ADD in my physiological evaluation.

My aunt looked at the counselor and said, "Do you realize my niece is not ADD? It says she has traits of ADD and there are traits in everybody on earth. You have them, I have them, and the president of the U.S.A. has them."

The counselor began to stutter, saying how she was just trying to help.

My aunt responded, "How? This could follow her for the rest of her life. Please explain to me how this helps her?"

Bottom line is my school was caught red handed and had not expected to have a child present in the school with educated family members. I was relieved to know I wasn't crazy. I had been tricked into signing something, and I made every other child that had signed the form aware that they also had been tricked into signing something that falsely diagnosed them as being ADD.

Of course, it caused uproar in the school. Not only did hell break loose for the school principal and counselor, but it backfired on me, as well. As I stated previously, I was a pretty good student. I had no failing grades and was getting ready to graduate. The principal pulled me into his office one day from my college prep class, where we filled out applications for college and wrote our college essays, to tell me that I should probably not try to become a doctor, but they could get me into a really good medical assistant program. He felt I would be good at that.

I sat in that chair thinking I could be a doctor, but he kept ministering death to every dream I had until I broke down. That evening, I went home thinking I was so stupid. *He's right. I'm not college material,* I thought. *Maybe I should become a medical assistant.*

At that point, I wanted to leave that school, but I had the threat of my father riding my brainwaves like a horse. So, I felt trapped. I could hear my dad in my ear: *If you get kicked out of this school or you mess up, that's it. I wash my hands of you.*

I suffered the abuse of that school for as long as I could. Every day I was pulled from my college prep class to be told how I wasn't ready for Corporate America.

The straw that broke the camel's back for me was when graduation time rolled around. My grades said that I could graduate, but the principal said I couldn't. He said to me, "I know you were supposed to graduate this August, but I am not confident that you're ready for the world. So, we're going to let you graduate with the second graduating class." I screamed in tears in his office, cussing him out and calling him every name but the name that his parents gave him. He had broken me down for the last time. I wanted out of there.

I ran to the main office and told them I quit. I didn't care about any threats my father made. The office administrator tried to warn me of something, but I was so upset that I couldn't even hear her correctly. She said, "Armetria, please listen to me. STAY! Don't go! He has screwed up the transcripts of everyone that has tried to leave here, causing them problems in whatever school they chose to attend. Armetria, trust me… please trust me on this. STAY PUT!"

Now, I wish I had listened, but back then, I was emotionally bruised, offended, bitter, and REJECTED. I ran and left the school, only to enroll in another school that wanted to put me in the eleventh grade. I fell to the floor and cried before those people. "No, that can't be true," I said. "I was graduating this year. I was in the twelfth grade!"

The administrator of the new school told me to go back to my old school and have them fix my transcripts. I did just that, but he only fixed my transcript enough to have me do another year in the twelfth grade.

I had no advocate in my new school. Just like he said, my dad had washed his hands. So, I was now responsible for myself. With my transcript being so messed up, they said I had to do an additional year because they had made a mistake of having me take too many classes that I didn't need, while neglecting the other classes that would have given me the credits needed to graduate. By now, I'd had enough. I gave up! I quit! I ended up dropping out of high school and instead attended night school years later to obtain my high school diploma at the age of twenty-four years old, scoring in the top 5% in the country on the Who's Who Among America's Top High School Students. And all while pregnant with my third child.

Presently, my maternal grandmother continues to reject me. My uncle that I mentioned above would molest and penetrate me over and over again. I could never talk about it because I knew she wouldn't believe me. Well, maybe I should say that she simply wouldn't accept the truth and find a way to blame me. So, I beat her to the punch! I felt I should allow him to abuse me repeatedly because my mother abandoned me and I was occupying his room.

When I turned twenty-four years old, the rape which I endured by the hands of her son was revealed to my grandmother, and to this day, she has verbalized that she hates me, wishes she had never taken me in, and doesn't want me in her life.

What rejection to receive from your own grandmother! Once my mom found out and we had a conversation about it, I told her it was true that her little brother had molested me. Yet, I experienced more rejection because she asked me to just not talk about it.

Reflections

Rejection and abandonment run hand in hand; yet, they are a little different. Abandonment is different from rejection in the sense that anyone can be rejected and will suffer from some rejection in their lifetime. Abandonment is rejection by someone who should be there for you. (Heb. 13:5) Abandonment is basically the action, and the rejection is the emotions and reaction that follows behind that.

I dealt with this void and lived with it, if you want to call it living. I wasn't living at all, though. I was a lost cause, lost in my emotion and in the locked places of my mind. It made me very skeptical of people. I was always wondering if someone was out to get me or ready to get over on me. I couldn't take constructive criticism either; I would think you were judging me. My broken, crushed emotions would throb every time I thought of doing anything great.

The spirit of abandonment is meant to destroy you and cause you to kill good relationships. It can begin all because of the belief in the lie that you must destroy it or abandon a person before they abandon you. It turned me into a quitter. I gave up on dreams and visions I had for myself. I would start something exciting and new, and then quit out of fear of nobody else standing in agreement with me. I would also find myself apologizing for things that weren't even my fault.

One of the most prevalent lies I found that the enemy will shoot to your heart is 'You are unlovable, you are not wanted, and you didn't live up to your end of things.' The enemy's job is to wear you out in the people-pleasing department and cause an emotional tsunami.

You have authority over the spirit of rejection and abandonment, just like I had authority. When I started asserting my authority and counteracting the lies with the truth, my life began to change and I was able to see major differences. Many of us have suffered abandonment by way of death, divorce, disaster, betrayal, and simply neglect. Close friends become separated, spouses betrayed, children are left to dry. You may find yourself isolated, hopeless, helpless, and with damaged feelings.

I have come to remind you that although we have suffered rejection and abandonment from man, God wants us to know He will never leave nor forsake us. We are the called righteousness of God through Christ Jesus and have been adopted into a family that we will never be released from.

Healing Balm for the Soul

"I will not leave you as orphans: I will come to you. Before long, the world will not see me anymore, but you will see me. Because I live, you also will live. On that day you will realize that I am in my Father, and you are in me, and I am in you."

John 14:18

"For as many as are led by the Spirit of God, these are the sons of God. For you did not receive the spirit of bondage again to fear, but you received the Spirit of adoption by whom we cry out, 'Abba, Father.' The Spirit bears witness with our spirit that we are children of God."

Romans 8:14-16

A Love Letter to You

Beloved,

What a journey we're on! I am excited and proud of you for taking this journey with Father and me. You are such a precious child of the King and the Most High God. He wants you to know that no matter who has rejected or abandoned you, he has never left your side. He says every tear you've cried he has collected them in the palm of his hands as he comforted your heart and gave you rest. Remember that Abba is a term of endearment and closeness, similar to "daddy." You are not God's foster child. You are His child, and all the intimacy that it suggests is yours if you will take it. Until we meet again here on earth or when we are connected to play together in Heaven, I love you and so does Abba. Be released to love and care for yourself. (Phil 1:6)

Lovingly,
Armetria

A JOURNEY TO SELF LOVE

The Fear Trap

Chapter 3

ARMETRIA M. CHARLES

The Fear Trap

I was afraid of everything: the dark, the Bible, the Lord, opportunities, spirits, any and everything imaginable. My fear was so deep that it had strong roots that had more roots. It was really tormenting. My first encounter with an overwhelming amount of fear was when I was about six years old. My mother would allow me to watch movies that instilled fear, like *Nightmare on Elm Street*, *Halloween*, and *Poltergeist*. You name the scary flick of the 80's and I probably watched it. I strongly believe I was allowed to watch these movies so she could use them as forms of control and manipulation over me.

One specific encounter I remember as if it were yesterday was having a real challenge writing one of the letters in my name backwards. My mother was working with me to get it right. At first, she was encouraging me and trying to help me get it correct. That soon changed when I became even more challenged and couldn't seem to get it right. That's when she began yelling at me, which only made me more nervous. So, I kept making the same mistakes. When I began to whine about not being able to do it, she grabbed me, took me to the linen closet, tossed me inside, and locked me in the bitter darkness.

"I don't care if Freddy Krueger's mother comes in and get you!" she started yelling.

I screamed and screamed, banged and kicked for her to let me out. I felt a tremendous amount of fear completely take over my mind and body. My little body was overtaken by something I couldn't understand, and I felt like I was going to blackout. Eventually, after making a promise that I would get the lettering right, she released me from the dark closet, but the torment stayed within.

I remember sitting there terrified as a little child and completely not able to comprehend the mental abuse I had just suffered. My hands shook as I struggled to get the letters correct in my name. Although I can't remember if that was ever done again, it was the beginning of a journey filled with fear and a seemingly undying torment.

I feared practically everything. Because of that experience, I would often hallucinate, thinking I saw things in the dark that weren't there. However, in my mind, the boogie man was real and very present. I feared what people thought of me. In my mind, I had preconceived that they thought I was not important and nobody wanted to help me.

I grew up in total fear of my mother, as she never seemed to have much control in the way she would try to get a point across. I was always called horrible names, especially the female dog name. I was hit and beaten so much that even when she wasn't after me to chastise/abuse me, I would approach her ducking and throwing my hands up, thinking she would find some reason to hit me.

My mother was a master liar and she forced me to become one, too. That behavior would make me afraid to voice my opinion or even ask for things. One day, I was playing with a little girl that lived upstairs from us, and her mom had prepared lunch for her to eat. My mom had not fed me and I was really hungry. In my mind, I wanted to ask the girl's mom if I could have some food, too, but I was too afraid. So, I sat there as my friend finished up her lunch and the smell of beef Ramen noodles traveled up my nose, causing my belly to flip in excitement and anticipation. I was thinking I was going to be filled with some, too.

I tried so hard to express through my facial expressions that I wanted my friend's mom to offer me some noodles. She didn't! When her mom left us in the living room to play, I asked my friend to tell her mom that she was still hungry and wanted more food so I could have something to eat, as well. The interesting thing is that my childlike lies had not fooled the mother at all. As she approached me with an attitude, I could feel my fear meter go from scared to terrified in ten seconds.

"If you want something to eat, ASK! I know my daughter, and she does not eat two packs of noodles. Did your mother feed you this morning?"

I continued the lie, thinking I would be in trouble if my mom found out. Besides, I was just simply embarrassed, so I ate nothing. Fear caused me to go without food for that period time.

My nana (paternal grandmother) would come and bring bags of food and a little pocket change every other weekend or so while my dad was incarcerated. She would ask me if I was alright and I would always say yes, when truth was I was not alright. I was terrified of my mother; she scared the hell out of me literally. My mom would constantly warn me that if I ever told the truth about her to others, I would be taken away and placed in a home where I would be treated worse. She'd call it the Sasha Bruce House or a reform school. She had really done a mental work on me, so I wouldn't say anything to anyone revealing who she really was for fear of being placed in a worse situation. I used to urinate on myself often, and everyone thought I had a weak bladder. After a while, I would urinate on myself because of that reason.

When my dad and mom were somewhat together, they would fight all the time. It terrified me to the point that if any other man would place his hands on my mom to hurt her, I would be stuck to him like white on rice. With my dad, I was terrified to break them up or jump in. I had always been a daddy's girl and I would never hurt my dad. Sometimes I would hear them fighting, and it seemed he would be beating her so bad I thought he would kill her. I could never rid myself of the echoes of her cries, as they haunted my very being.

Sometimes I used to sneak and call the cops, and they would show up asking questions. My mom would lie out of fear and say everything was alright. When the police officers would look at me and ask if I called, I would lie and say no. I just wanted them to stop fighting. They frightened me, and as mean as my mom could be, I never wanted to see her hurt. I would scream at my father, "Daddy, please stop! STOP!" He would look at me with these red eyes of fire and then tell me to go back to my room. I would hope and pray he stopped beating her.

One day, my mother used me to provoke my dad to anger. They were fussing over something pertaining to them cheating on one another. I think my mom started it. My dad tried to leave, and because she knew I was the apple of his eye, she used me to provoke him. As he was almost down the hall outside of our apartment, my mother grabbed me, tripped me up, placed her foot on my chest, and started yelling down the hall to my dad.

Under the pressure of her foot, I started to yell, "Daddy, Daddy!"

My father turned around and ran back up the hallway. I thought he was going to kill her! I think he hit her in the head with something. I screamed for him to stop to try and save her. After he finished beating on her, she began crying. Her head was split open in the middle and bloody.

"See what you did?" she sobbed to me. I remember the overwhelming feeling of fear and guilt because I believed it was entirely my fault.

Funny that the closet my mother used to torment me would also be used to torment the both of us one day. Allow me to introduce you to my mother's psycho, drug dealer boyfriend, Caesar, who terrorized our home one night. Well, I don't know what happened exactly, but I think she had stolen his drug stash.

She and her druggie crew were in the dining room smoking up a storm. The apartment was thick with clouds of crack cocaine smoke. They weren't concerned at all about me sitting there inhaling that poison. Well, I remember one person asked her, "What about your daughter sitting in there?" My mother replied, "Awww, that's my baby girl, my firstborn. She knows what's up."

They continued to smoke, when a loud knock echoed through the apartment. I mean, it was loud. That knock made the earth stand still as its intent was to stop everything, and it did.

While my heart skipped beats, I remember feeling like something wasn't right in my little spirit. I heard the addicts scattering around to hide, especially my mother. They started whispering, and my mother convinced someone to ask who it was.

"Who is it?" the woman asked, and he replied, "Caesar." My mother was signaling for her to tell him that she wasn't there. So, the woman yelled out, "Angie's not here." However, he demanded that she open the door or else.

My mother knew this man hated me, and she couldn't leave me out in the open allowing him access to me. Therefore, she grabbed and shoved me in the dark closet that she had used many times to torment me. With her teeth clinched tightly together and her mouth barely moving, she told me, "If you breathe, sneeze, or talk, I will kill you."

My mother stands about six feet tall. We were hiding behind a small Christmas tree while Caesar and his accomplice perused our home with guns. I know the guns were huge because I heard the addicts' comments outside the closet as they stuttered while explaining my mom wasn't home. The woman who answered the door was asked "Where is Angie?" and fearfully, she replied, "I don't know. She was just here. She had to have jumped out the window or something, because she was just here." When he asked, "Where's her daughter?" my eyes got huge.

I remembered asking my mother about God in past conversations, and she would always respond in some sarcastic way. Maybe she didn't know the answers. I would ask, "Momma, what color is God?" She'd answer, "He's every color." I'd ask, "Momma, is God a man or woman?" She'd reply, "He's both. Why do you ask so many questions?"

Apparently, I had heard or read about a God that answered prayers somewhere, because although my momma told me to be quiet or be killed, I went against the grain to approach a God I knew nothing about. I uttered these words in this exact order: "God, if you're real, please make me and my mother invisible."

The searching and the ruckus continued outside of the closet door, while another woman asked, "Why y'all gotta come in here with those big guns, man?" Caesar told her to mind her business. I guess she was really high, because everyone else was probably too afraid to speak, leave, or ask questions. She looked at the other guy and asked him, "Aren't you so-n-so's son?" He didn't answer her, but began talking to Caesar, saying, "Man, she knows my father. Man, let's go! You'll catch up to her later!"

Caesar wasn't giving up because my mother had done something. It was something bad and she knew it. I could feel the heat and smell the crack on my mother's breath. He came near the closet, opened the door, and closed it. He did not come inside to see if we were hiding there. At that point, I was a believer. God was real!

Later on, we heard that Caesar was murdered in the Sursum Corda Housing Project. I know that if he had gotten to me or my mother, we would be dead. Thank you, Lord, for sparing me and my mom! Later, in that dreadful place I called home, my mother would rent out her room to two dope heads.

Renée and Block were their names. They had a little baby girl that I loved to play with and care for. Besides, Block and Renée were always high or sleep. It seemed to me that dope would make them sleep for days. Whenever the baby cried, I would go and get milk to feed her, burp her, and then put her back to sleep as if she were mine.

Early one day — and I mean early in the morning — I heard the baby crying and I started to get up to get her. My mother woke up and asked, "Where are you going?" I said, "To get the baby," and she replied, "That's not your (curse word) baby. Lay back down." I did as I was told, and just laid there wanting desperately to help, play with, and make the baby happy. Her cries started to concern me. I thought my mother was so mean. I remember thinking that Renée and Block would never hear her. So, I asked, "Momma, can I go and wake Renée and Block up?" But, she told me, "No. Lay back down."

That poor baby cried for the longest time. I mean, it had to be at least an hour. After a while, the baby stopped crying. I couldn't help but override my mother's instructions not to rescue or be concerned about the baby. As I started to climb over my mom, she asked again, "Where are you going?" I replied with a lie, telling her, "I have to use the bathroom."

I did go to the bathroom to make what I told my mother the truth in case she asked me if I used it. Still, I crept off into Renée and Block's room to see my little baby doll, and to my surprise, the baby was laying there with her eyes wide open and tongue hanging out. She had died of SID's. I screamed to the top of my lungs as my mother hopped up to see what had happened. Block and Renée still had not awakened. My mother had to shake them violently. Finally, Renée started screaming and crying. I just knew it was all my fault. I should have saved that baby.

Sure, I lied the second time, but felt I should have lied the first time to relieve her of her crying. To this day, I can't stand to hear a baby cry. The fear seeds that were sown had started to grow and play a major role in my life as a teenager and adult. When people asked me questions, I would lie and tell them what they wanted to hear out of fear. Always afraid of rejection and hurt, it was hard for me to love anyone.

In my mind, everybody was an enemy. I would go to take exams at school and be terrified that I would miss the whole test. I was so consumed with how afraid I was to fail that I wouldn't even get started. I was afraid to sleep without some sort of light as a child, teenager, and adult. Up to my mid-twenties, I was afraid of prayer closets. When I would hear people say "Go into your prayer closet," it would set me off. I would become overwhelmed with torment. Therefore, I couldn't enjoy a real relationship with Christ. Instead, it was only an acknowledgement of His existence.

I use to always fear that something bad was going to happen to the people close to me. So, I never wanted to be really close to anyone. Reading the Bible when it got deep would run me away. I had become fearful in a tormenting way of the Lord. My life was consumed and controlled by a stronghold of fear, and I never felt I was good enough. Butterflies would overwhelm my tummy when asking simple questions like "May I have something to eat?"

I believe my overwhelming spirit of fear killed a major part of the relationship with my father. He always said I could be straight up with him, but due to fear, I questioned his sincerity.

For a long time, I was afraid to sleep alone; I always felt that something was going to grab me. In relationships, I always felt that people would betray me or abandon me. In school and life, I would never step up to the plate because I was afraid I would fail.

I was a master procrastinator, and later on, I would trace those roots to fear. Because of fear, I could never complete anything, have courageous conversations, or verbalize if someone hurt me or my feelings. Here is an interesting behavioral pattern I discovered about myself. I would sweep trash into a pile and never remove the pile. I just seemed to be really incomplete and felt that I was a spiritual hermit crab.

Reflections

The dominant spirit here was fear, and it packed a serious blow of torment. I was fearful, and it was a tormenting fear that controlled every area of my life. The emotional torment sometimes made me contemplate suicide. I felt somehow that I would experience some peace there. That was a piece of evidence of the torment I suffered. Fear is a silent killer. So, if we are quiet about our sufferings, then we allow the enemy to win.

Fear is used by the enemy to keep us from having all that God wants for us, which are the things the enemy is afraid for you to have possession of — you having access to the very things that will defeat and destroy him. He wanted me silenced! If he could convince me I wasn't meant to speak or share because what I experienced was shameful, I wouldn't be able to minister to you right now. I've learned that none of this was really about me, but about you and the countless others I will touch through my experiences.

The enemy isn't really into attacking people; he is after your purpose. Be careful what you listen to. The word says that faith comes by hearing, but fear and negativity also comes by hearing. Pay close attention because the enemy will always say you are the opposite of what you are. He may say you are a loser, and that's because he knows you are a winner. He knows if you ever grabbed hold of that champion's mindset, he would have no power over you. So, he's more afraid of us than we should ever be of him.

What was really interesting to me was the very place that God tells us to visit (the prayer closet) was the place that terrified me most. Look at your life and think about some of the things you have heard within or through others, and then think about yourself on the opposite side of the spectrum. The enemy says you're fat; you say you're healthy. He says you should be quiet because people won't listen; that's the time to talk it out because people are waiting to be set free from your message. He creates fear about you going to the next level; you push yourself to go, because anywhere there is success the enemy will counterfeit it with fear.

He has been a liar and a thief from the very beginning. His job is to steal, kill, and destroy. Isn't it interesting that he must first steal before he can kill our spirits and ultimately destroy us? Now that you are aware of his tactics, will you step out on faith and begin the process of living your life in and on purpose? You are who God says you are, and that means the opposite of what the enemy says.

Healing Balm for the Soul

Meditate on these scriptures deeply. Say them, mutter them, think about them continuously, ponder them, and declare them in the first person. They are weapons to defeat that evil demon of fear which is designed to stop you from doing the will of our Father in heaven and living your best life.

For God has not given us a spirit of fear, but of power and of love and of a sound mind.

2 Timothy 1:7

There is no fear in love; but perfect love casts out fear, because fear involves torment. But he who fears has not been made perfect in love.

1 John 4:18

The LORD is my light and my salvation; whom shall I fear? The LORD is the strength of my life; of whom shall I be afraid?

Psalm 27:1

Have I not commanded you? Be strong and of good courage; do not be afraid, nor be dismayed, for the LORD your God is with you wherever you go.

Joshua 1:9

I am the God of your father Abraham; do not fear, for I am with you.

Genesis 26:24

A Love Letter to You

Beloved,

Be released from the bondage of untruths. Be set free from the fear that binds you. You are powerful beyond measure. You are a designer's original, a masterpiece! Don't allow faithless seeds of fear to be implanted in your souls, because your soul is only fit for seeds of holiness. Guard the avenues of your soul by not allowing people that don't walk according to the spirit to minister what you can and cannot do in your life. Remember, you can do all things through Christ that strengthens you. I stand in agreement with you that you will have an intentional, on purpose, and faith-filled life. Now, go reflect on the beauty and love that we find in God, our Father. There's nothing to fear because God is always in control. I believe in you. Now it's your turn to believe in you. Be strong and courageous. That's a direct command from Father. (Joshua 3:1-9)

Lovingly,
Armetria

A JOURNEY TO SELF LOVE

Counterfeit Love

Chapter 4

Armetria M. Charles

Counterfeit Love

Growing up, I wished my dad and I were a lot closer. I believe there was a time when he really admired me, but that was when I was a baby girl. My daddy was my hero, my protector, my everything. Then abruptly, he was taken away from me due to prison sentences. Even though there was such space between us, I knew he loved me without a shadow of a doubt.

During most of my dad's jail sentencing, I lived with my maternal grandmother who couldn't stand him. I never knew why she didn't like him. She never had a valid reason to give me. My grandmother was famous for using my dad's absence as a form of verbal abuse by telling me, "You don't have a father. I am your father." I experienced a lot of hurt from people because of my father not being there to protect me.

I always felt he missed out on so much in my life, and all of it was detrimental to me. I needed his protection and I needed his shelter. I was able to live with him after a bitter struggle with my grandmother who did not want to let me go. She would complain all of the time about how she wanted to get rid of me, but then when my father wanted me, she wouldn't let me go. I know it was because if she let me go, that meant no more food stamps and cash benefits from welfare. My father's family continued to ask her for me and even told her that she could keep the money she got from welfare, but she still wouldn't release me.

    I loved and wanted to see my dad so much that when she would send me to school on the bus, I would take my bus token that would get me home and ride an extra eight minutes on another bus to sneak and see him. I would always catch him and my nana, and they would drop me back off at school. My maternal grandmother found out because the school began to call regarding my attendance and punctuality. I always felt it would take more than distance to keep me away from the man I loved unconditionally. I was an awesome student and made really good grades, but that started to fail knowing my dad was home and I couldn't be with him. I started getting into fights, not doing my work, and even began looking to my male teachers for affection. All of this was because I missed and so badly longed for my dad.

    I had a male teacher in fourth grade named Mr. McKantz, and he loved the Lord with all his heart. He even taught me some things about the Lord. I admired him. He always dressed nice and smelled great. He was tall, dark, and handsome I didn't have a crush on him. He simply reminded me of my father. I would always find a reason to hug or hang up under Mr. McKantz, and that began to concern him. He made a visit to my home and explained it to my maternal grandmother who was furious with me. I still couldn't quite comprehend what I had done wrong. It was explained to me that I was too clingy, which is not a good look for a male teacher and his female student.

    My grandmother continued to receive complaints about me, and when my mother came back from one of her five-month crack excursions, my grandmother had her beat me as usual. The painful part about the beatings were I didn't even really know this woman that came to see me every five months to beat me and do my hair. Also, I couldn't draw the connection as to why I was being beaten like a man on the street. I went to school the next day and got into more trouble. Again, my grandmother summoned my mother to do what she did best...abuse me! Even my mom was tired of beating me this time and asked me what my problem was.

    I said, "I want to live with my daddy."

My grandmother started saying how stupid I was and how I wasn't going anywhere.

Well, my mother replied, "If that's where she wants to be, let her go live with that (curse word) then."

Without a call or a notice, my mother and grandmother packed many of my things, and my mother dropped me off on the doorstep of my nana's home. She told me, "Don't move. I don't care if Jesus comes. Don't move until your father or grandmother gets here."

My nana worked and wouldn't get home until maybe 6:00 p.m., and it was early afternoon when I was dropped off. So, I sat there for a few hours until my grandmother (paternal) pulled up in her Woody's smock after a long hard day of work.

She walked up to the step, her eyes full of my bags of clothing, and asked, "What are you doing up here? Your other grandmother knows you're here?"

I answered back, "Yes, she knows, but my momma brought me here to live with you."

My nana helped me gather my things and her next words were, "You hungry?"

I replied, "Yes," and that was the beginning of me residing with my nana and dad.

I wanted a closer relationship with my dad, but fear played a part in how I communicated with him. He always seemed to be in a big hurry or a rush to get somewhere or to see someone. I would often miss him. If I had something to say, I had better said it quickly…and I mean quick because he could be leaving while you were in mid sentence. I longed for the closeness and unconditional love from a father. Although I saw my dad and we would hang out sometimes, I felt his attention was always divided. One thing I can say about my dad is he would see to it that I received roses and cards on Valentine's Day and birthdays, which meant a lot. Still, there was so much missing. I wanted to be able to talk to him freely about any and everything, and I still couldn't do that. I sought that in someone else.

I will never forget the summer when I was fourteen years old and met this guy on a bike. I'm not sure what I saw, but I was just being a flirt. He liked me, also. We ended up getting into a VERY unhealthy relationship. The relationship was built on lies which started from the very beginning when he told me that he was seventeen years old. Come to find out he was in his mid twenties. By the time I found out, it was too late. I thought I was in love. He bought me whatever I wanted and made time for just ME! He picked me up and dropped me off at school, and on the weekends, we were together. We were ALWAYS together. It was very unhealthy. I was still a child and in a dangerous counterfeit love relationship with a man.

My father was somewhat against it, but he was a little too busy to attend to it. He would make comments that let me know he was not very happy with my selection, but he continued to live as usual. So, I also lived. I stayed in this relationship to find out this man was a drug dealer, carried lots of guns, and eventually had become abusive towards me. I ended up pregnant and forced into a marriage with him where we had two beautiful boys. After moving past that, I continued the path to entangle myself with many counterfeit lovers. I paid the price all because I was looking for love in all the wrong places.

I remember the emotional rape of being with a man just because I needed a warm body next to me or to have some security in saying I had a man. I was everybody's boo and nobody's bride! There were moments I would just lay there to allow a man to enter me, while my mind and spirit were not even there. I forced myself to do it all because I was looking for a love I would never find until I found real love in the Lord and my dynamic husband, Frederick A. Charles.

Reflections

How many of us have looked for love in all the wrong places? The very thing that seems so right ends up being so wrong. That was once me. I had been in a relationship trying to grab hold of all the things I felt I missed with my dad, and I ended up getting an even shorter end of the stick. I was reaching out for help and couldn't seem to find it. It wasn't the material things that I was looking for, but the emotional protection, shelter, and support that only my father could provide at that point in my life. I thought these benefits were accessible in a person or a partner. Boy was I wrong! Later, I would find that only God could fill these kinds of voids. Different situations may have us looking for love and acceptance in all the wrong places. Searching but never finding as we dig ourselves into a deeper emotional hole of self hate. I found out that we can save so much wasted time by looking to God and coming to the understanding that unless we have found Him and the man that we are with has found Him, the love that's shared will always be COUNTERFEIT.

Ask yourself, why do I love him or her? Do I really love him or her, or am I just holding on to the one thing I couldn't find in one of my parents? If I am shacking up with a man or woman, why is it that I do this? What feelings am I looking for? Is it going to go anywhere? If that man or woman loves you, let him honor you by loving you like Christ loved the church. Allow him to make you an honored woman.

Maybe you are one who seeks the love of your father or mother in your husband or wife. Well, allow me to inform you that these expectations of your mate are unfair! He or she is your husband or your wife and have not been placed in your life to govern a parental role, but to participate as a spouse. Many times we will even inflict pain on our spouses because others have hurt us, especially when hurt is caused by our parents. Ask yourself, do I rely on him or her to make up for what my father or mother did or didn't do? Am I holding my husband or wife accountable for some hurt I've experienced through a counterfeit lover in the past? If your answer is yes to either of those questions, it's time for a spiritual release!

Repeat: I have all the love I need in Jesus! I am emotionally whole through Jesus. He loves me unconditionally, and I am worth being honored and extending honor to others.

Healing Balm for the Soul

Such hope never disappoints or deludes or shames us, for God's love has been poured out in our hearts through the Holy Spirit who has been given to us.
Romans 5:5

And I will sow her for Myself anew in the land, and I will have love, pity, and mercy for her who had not obtained love, pity, and mercy; and I will say to those who were not My people, You are My people, and they shall say, You are my God!
Hosea 2:23

I pray that out of his glorious riches he may strengthen you with power through his Spirit in your inner being, so that Christ may dwell in your hearts through faith. And I pray that you, being rooted and established in love, may have power, together with all the saints, to grasp how wide and long and high and deep is the love of Christ, and to know this love that surpasses knowledge-that you may be filled to the measure of all the fullness of God. Now to him who is able to do immeasurably more than all we ask or imagine, according to his power that is at work within us, to him be glory in the church and in Christ Jesus throughout all generations, forever and ever! Amen!
Ephesians 3:16-21

A Love Letter to You

Beloved,

Wow, wow, wow! I am thrilled at how much God is in love with you. You have never felt a love like this because it's simply not based on a feeling, but a truth! God's love for you runs deep. Not even the closest loved one can compare to it. God's love for you is everlasting and unchanging, as he would lay down his life for the love of you. God wants you to know you don't have to go searching. The searching can stop right here and right now because he has loved you with an undying love from the very beginning. Access him in his holy word and through prayer while dwelling on how much he loves you. He says no matter what you've done or what others have done to you, you and him can never be separated. For you are bound by true love from the one and only true God we call our Father. (Romans 8:35-39)

Lovingly,
Armetria

A JOURNEY TO SELF LOVE

The Key To Accepting Me

Chapter 5

ARMETRIA M. CHARLES

The Key to Accepting Me

I remember always needing an entourage just so I would never be forced to be alone. I always had a bunch of people in my home, which was the hangout spot because I simply never wanted to be alone. I had a serious issue with people-pleasing, and I paid a heavy price for that. I'd hang around people that were far from who I really was and what I ever wanted to be. However, those were the only people willing to hang with me in my condition. I was often influenced by these people, finding myself in nightclubs dancing, drinking, and sometimes even smoking. Wow, this was far from me, but I wanted so badly to fit in a crowd where I was allowed to be comfortable in my mess.

Taking a look down memory lane, I remember my mother saying, "You buy your friends." Did I? Would I bribe people into being my friend because I was a people pleaser? I think I can pinpoint where this may have come from. My mother went from being a wonderful mom, a role model, and someone I had always wanted to be like to a crack addict, abuser, and a person I would never want to be like. I was always forced to convince myself and others that I was better off than I was.

I remember hearing the kids in school teasing me because my mother was on drugs. "Your mother is on crack. I saw her hitting the pipe last night." Or, "Don't play with Armetria. She has AIDS." It would crush me.

Such lies of cruelty. I was always looking to find people I didn't know so I could create an illusion of everything I was not. If you didn't know me, I would tell you that my parents were big-shot successful people simply because I wanted to fit in. I never really thought about being molested or abused much because I was taught to save face.

Living with my maternal grandmother was a very funny thing. We lived in the projects, yet she made us think we were the best thing since sliced bread. We were better dressed, cared for, and classier than everyone else. So, when I grew up, I learned to segregate people based on where they lived and how they looked. That didn't last for long because of all the self-esteem issues I carried. My hunger to be accepted took over. I would be willing to hang with the most ghetto folks just to be accepted. I wasn't accepted there either, though. I was always asked, "Why do you talk like that?" Or, "Why do you act like that?" I think I knew what they meant. My grandmother didn't allow slang talk in her home and I was very sheltered. Although I suffered a great deal, she taught me to be a lady: crossed legs, learned mannerisms, and keep my outer appearance in tact even if I felt like crap. Never leave the house without your earrings and everything matching from undergarments to the outer ones. I was not allowed outside. Books and movies were my only link to the outside world. Here's the kicker with that, none of the stuff I read or watched was my reality. So, I created a fantasy life of my own around it. In my sheltered mind, I was one of the Cosby's kids. Pollyanna and I had it going on. Then, in another world, it was completely opposite. I was in the ghetto. I was a chameleon. I could hang with the classiest of folks, speak and deal on their level, and then deal with the class of the hood.

Once I had gotten everyone to believe I was better off than anyone would ever imagine, something would happen to shed light on the truth. I would then be embarassed and retreat, looking for another crowd to be a part of. I was always the class clown, always in trouble for talking in class and making everyone laugh. People laughing at me and not with me was all right because it meant in some form that I had been accepted by them.

With all of the different trend styles, I had to have everything that came out to keep up with the people I was trying to impress. Half of the stuff I would beg my father to buy me I didn't even like, but I knew my peers would, and as a result, I would be the highlight of conversation.

It really began to place a huge damper on my integrity, commitments, and more importantly, my word. I would join a cause that I had no real interest in just to please others. I burned a lot of bridges by wearing myself out trying to please everyone. I suppose because I was always competing for attention, and was seriously neglected in a lot of areas, I would look for acceptance. It made me out to become a liar, a criminal, and a cheat.

I started hanging with a young lady from my junior high school who one day decided to teach me to steal. Not that I didn't already know how to steal. She was just a pro. She promised me friendship, and because I honored having her as a friend, I followed her lead to leave school one day and visit the mall. We went in to Nordstrom's Rack and 'racked' up. I watched as she would rip the security tag off of anything she wanted. The first go around, I was scared and nervous. I didn't get anything. She thought I was such a punk. When we went back another day, I began to steal shoes and jewelry. It didn't end there, though. It was fun hanging with her and being accepted, but later on, I would realize that was not real friendship or acceptance. I was being used. She had someone crazy and dumb enough to go with her. Me! The third time we went to Nordstrom's Rack would be the last. We were apprehended, and she blamed everything on me. We were hauled off to jail where my nana came to rescue me as usual. By this time, I was residing with my nana and father. My father was so incredibly disenchanted. I was in big trouble and I felt the heat, trust me. Nordstrom's sued my dad for the items that both the young lady and I had stolen.

You would think I had learned my lesson, but I didn't. The hunger to be accepted grew stronger and stronger. By the time I hit my first year of high school, I was hanging with the wrong crowd again. The bunch was a mixture and everyone had a boyfriend. So, I figured I'd grab one of those, too. My new friends were having sex, so I figured I'd do it, as well. Soon, I would be adopted into an unofficial gang with a group of girls. That was the most rewarding feeling to me. They really knew how to counterfeit love, and I was sold on it. We looked out for one another, and if someone wanted to fight one of us, they would see all of us.

One day, one of the girls in school involved me in some hearsay, and one of the leaders of our group said, "Armetria, you better get her before I do. It won't be pretty." I fell right into the trap. The rumor was another group of girls were supposed to jump us. So, we had to be prepared. The next day, the leaders and I were to attend ROTC, meaning we had to arrive to school by 6:00 a.m. That morning, I grab the biggest, fluffiest teddy bear I could find. I cut a hole in it and stuffed the stomach of the bear with all sorts of weapons, mainly knives.

Normally, you couldn't get into our school without being searched and going through the metal detectors, but with it being 6:00 a.m., there were no guards to search anyone since they weren't due to work until 7:45 a.m. However, someone ran off at the mouth, and later, we all were called to the office with the police present. They wanted to know about this Valentine's Day bear that held all of the weapons. We lied and said there were no weapons. When the police took us all separately to our lockers to do a thorough search, the bear was found in the gang leader's locker.

The code of conduct was to keep your mouth shut no matter what. I did, but as we sat nervously in that office with sweat pouring off of us, the leader of our gang was asked, "Who does the bear belong to?" She said, "The bear belongs to Armetria. She brought it to school." My heart fell to my knees. I thought to myself, *What on earth? How could she snitch on me? She knows better.* We were never caught with the weapons I brought because she hid them in the locker of one of the special education students!

The police grabbed the bear and began inspecting it. I was literally falling apart within, experiencing a total mental meltdown. All of a sudden, I wished I was a loner instead of being a part of some crazy all-girl gang clique.

After that ordeal, I wanted out! Being a part of the gang was rewarding emotionally, but at the same time, it was mentally draining. I didn't like the drama that went along with the feeling of acceptance. Getting out was very hard because you just don't up and quit a gang. I ended up getting into fight after fight with the leader and other girls in the group. Eventually, my dad had to intervene. The price of acceptance was higher than I wanted to pay and more than I could afford to.

Not being accepted in a motherly way from my mom and grandmother, I longed to have that closeness with a mother figure. Every woman I was introduced to I called mommy, even though most of them could never handle the job. I was never really accepted by any of my dad's girlfriends because I was never really their child. I would always draw the contrast between me and the child(ren) they already had, and if I wasn't treated like them, I didn't feel included.

This made me think I wanted to be homosexual. I started hanging around women who were homosexual, thinking I could get the emotional piece that was missing from the women in my life fulfilled. Let me tell you, I could never bring myself to being sexual with another woman. I wanted the emotional connection, but not the sexual intimacy that came along with it. I was in a relationship with a female for about two weeks, and I would never let her touch me. I didn't care to be touched. I never even wanted to be seen with her. I simply wanted to use her for the emotional piece that was missing in my life. That relationship never worked out. I moved on quickly.

I continued my adult life people pleasing. Whatever people wanted, I provided. It drained me. Like I mentioned, the price was just too high for me to pay. I could never afford the debt of pleasing everyone. I continued living, seeking, searching, and longing for someone, anyone to just accept me, love me, embrace me, and never forsake me.

Reflections

I was seriously disrupted and taken advantage of by the spirit of needing to be accepted. It's an emotional and spiritual drainer. All that I worked for to be considered accepted, I ended up paying heavily with my peace, self-love, and self-esteem. The need to be accepted drove me into a place of hanging out with people I had no real desire to be with and going places I had no real desire to go. It led me to a place of feeling like I was a complete loser. The love and acceptance I fell for was a false copy of what God had in store for me. Mentally drained and sometimes left physically fatigued, I was ready to explore more options. I needed and wanted to be emotionally whole. My "Yes" to everything and everybody would cost me almost my life in most instances.

We don't recognize the danger we are in until we're in too deep. I didn't realize how serious it was to be involved in a gang until I was almost arrested and beaten so badly by the leaders who felt it was a lifetime initiation. If you are in agreement with the spirit of feeling and being accepted, I am calling you out now in the precious name of Yeshua (the sacred name of Jesus). This is not what God intended for my life or yours. You are the chosen one of God; you have already been accepted into a family and a relationship that doesn't cost you a thing, either mentally or emotionally, because Jesus already paid it all. There is only One to please, and in pleasing Him, you and all you come into contact with will be blessed.

I also found that when entangled with this need to be accepted and saying yes to everything, I never wanted to let people down. The reason being I never wanted anyone to leave my side. I couldn't speak my mind, and I would agree to things I knew I didn't agree with. I would nod my head yes to whatever made everyone else happy. I was a mess. This damage continued bad relationships and ended good ones, all because the bad ones continued to take advantage of me. I was spiritually killing myself trying to keep up with pleasing bad relationships. The good relationships in my life were challenged because I was promising things that I couldn't make good on. I was taking on duties that were far from my personal desires. The image of my word and my integrity was challenged, and in most cases, destroyed.

The people pleasing that comes along with the spirit of needing to be accepted is a very heavy price to pay, and it subtracts from the ability to love yourself completely and unconditionally. Release yourself from the need to say "YES" to everything and everyone. It's perfectly fine to say "NO" sometimes. No is not a dirty word. It will free you to protect your integrity and allow you to live a healthier, peaceful life in the freedom God intended, while subconsciously allowing others to respect your personal boundaries.

Healing Balm for the Soul

"*Having predestinated us unto the adoption of children by Jesus Christ to himself, according to the good pleasure of his will, to the praise of the glory of his grace, wherein he hath made us accepted in the beloved.*"

Ephesians 1:5-6

"*Whatever may be your task, work at it heartily (from the soul), as [something done] for the Lord and not for men, knowing [with all certainty] that it is from the Lord [and not from men] that you will receive the inheritance which is your [real] reward. [The One Whom] you are actually serving [is] the Lord Christ (the Messiah).*"

Colossians 3:23,24

"*But now we are discharged from the Law and have terminated all intercourse with it, having died to what once restrained and held us captive. So now we serve not under [obedience to] the old code of written regulations, but [under obedience to the promptings] of the Spirit in newness [of life].*"

Romans 7:6

A Love Letter to You

Beloved,

Breathe easy and rest assure that you have been indeed accepted and reconciled to Christ. He is the only being that you should work towards pleasing. The Holy Spirit of God desires to dwell within and direct your moves, decisions, and actions accordingly that you are ensured a holy protection. He wants to give you an indicator that will protect you from users and those who seek to scheme and abuse you.(Colossians 3:15) God is equipping you in your spirit to have peace about saying yes or no to things and people. How awesome is it to be so accepted by the Father that His one and only desire is to ensure your protection? You are completely secure in His arms. You are the beloved of Christ. Never forget that. God wants you to know He loves you and accepts you just as you are, flaws and all. He understands you, and therefore, He knows what is needed to heal, restore, and deliver you. Stay in the comfort of His arms. Although this may be a little challenging at first, He sent me to tell you that He will never leave nor forsake you. Now go and dance to the melodies of love towards God and the love you have towards yourself. *(Deuteronomy 31:6)*

Lovingly,
Armetria

A JOURNEY TO SELF LOVE

THE FAST BREAK FROM SELF PITY

Chapter 6

ARMETRIA M. CHARLES

The Fast Break from Self Pity

I feel so dirty, so nasty! Why does he do this to me? How could my mother allow strange men who would violate me to come into our home? I know she doesn't care; she never has. What pleasure could a grown man find in a skinny, bucktooth, little child?

I hated this with a passion! I hated the fact that I was taken advantage of! I know it was because she owed him money. When her drug dealers came knocking at the door, I was trained that I should reply, "My mother said she'll pay you on the first." Little did she know, the first wasn't the only payment they would be receiving. I was a prime target for abuse by these men who lacked any moral sense. Any person that would sell drugs to a woman with a child that is clearly devastated by the substance abuse is morally challenged.

I spent a great deal of time with other little girls whose mothers also smoked crack cocaine. We all ended up in the same prison of sexual abuse by our mothers' crack dealers or peers. I hated being taken advantage of, touched, breathed on, and violated by the same fat, funky guy. I will never forget that his name was Goon, and he was just that…a goon. I was so weak and vulnerable when he came around that I would melt in defenselessness. I felt weak, stupid, and helpless. Why wasn't I a fighter? I knew what he would make me do to him was wrong, but I let it happen. Perhaps I should have bit him, kicked him, something!

I was weak, just plain ole weak! There I was allowing someone to make me do what I knew in my heart was forbidden to do. My mouth was glued shut in any efforts of defending myself. Maybe that's the way it was supposed to be. Perhaps that's what happens all over the world in other girls' homes, and it's somehow okay. I was so uncomfortable with the nasty look in his eyes and the heaviness of his gross breathing. I felt stupid and weak for not being strong enough to stop him.

Reflections

In this chapter, I played around with self-pity. I felt and called myself weak. Perhaps this wasn't your situation; however, you have been in situations where you found yourself in a place of helplessness and self-pity. At the time, you were paralyzed in word and action, but mentally, you called yourself weak.

Due to the trauma of being violated in such a way, I blamed myself for not being able to stop the abuse. Some situations in our lives will leave us feeling like we don't have a voice. The little voice we have left is not strong enough to use towards self-edification or self-encouragement, yet it stands in total agreement with the underlying guilt of being helpless.

You may feel that you have allowed the doomsday DJ to play his favorite songs and #1 hits of foolishness in your head. We've danced to the beat of self-pity, harmonized with self-blame, and simply allowed that music to minister to us. It's now time to end these devastating parties and break those records and recording contracts over our lives forever.

Whatever the situations and circumstances, those conditions are not true for you now. You are no longer helpless. Devastation is and never was your fault, just as the events that went down in this chapter were due to no fault of my own. Who is ever prepared for someone to perform devastating acts against us? The answer is "NO ONE!" So, let's stop blaming ourselves for not having the tools to deal or cope with it. Right now, sister or brother, I am standing in agreement with you that the devastation of past assignments against you are canceled, in Jesus' name!

Healing Balm for the Soul

"Come to me, all who labor and are heavy laden, and I will give you rest. Take my yoke upon you, and learn from me, for I am gentle and lowly in heart, and you will find rest for your souls. For my yoke is easy, and my burden is light."
Matthew 11:28-30 (ESV)

I can do all things through him who strengthens me.
Philippians 4:13 (ESV)

But He was wounded for our transgressions, He was bruised for our iniquities; the chastisement for our peace was upon Him, and by His stripes we are healed.
Isaiah 53:5 (NKJV)

A Love Letter to You

Beloved,

How wonderful to know that you can shed the spirit of self-pity and blame because you can do all things through Christ who strengthens you. He has offered you rest from the spirit of heaviness of shame and guilt. You are completely healed because the chastisement for your peace was upon Him. Go and leap for joy in your spirit that Jesus knows how you feel and He has offered you a great release in Him.

Repeat after me:

I release myself from self pity.

I release myself from guilt.

I release myself from the effects of devastation.

I am empowered, fabulously blessed, and courageous.

The enemy is a conqueror, but God says you're more than that! (Roman 8:37)

Lovingly,

Armetria

A JOURNEY TO SELF LOVE

Forgiveness The Bitter Struggle

Chapter 7

Armetria M. Charles

Forgiveness: The Bitter Struggle

I once thought I had forgiven folks simply because that's what my mouth would say. I forgave him because I prayed for him. I forgave her because I wished her no harm. Truth is, I was deceived and hadn't forgiven anybody. The most painful memories I have stick to me like a tattoo. Like when my mother took cigarette matches and burned both my hands. That was her sick, twisted way of chastising me. The abuse from her was always extremely heavy and totally unnecessary. I was terrified of her due to brutal beatings with belts, extension cords, her hands, and anything her hands could grab. I simply feared her!

Once, her boyfriend had come to our home, and I was in her bed because she had given my room to some other addicts for rent money that never made it to the rental office. As I lay in her bed, I was happy to be next to my mom and experiencing some sense of affection because she was just simply there with me. No drugs, no men, no company, just the two of us. I lay there and pretended to be sleep, afraid this somewhat normal time would end if I let her see I was awake.

Sooner than later, her big-time drug dealer boyfriend, Caesar, knocked at the door. This man couldn't stand my guts, and frankly, I didn't like him either. Besides him not being my daddy, I always had this gift to be able to discern people that had evil spirits attached to them. I always thought he was a murderer or something, so he scared me. I shut my eyes a little tighter as Caesar came into the room. To his disappointment, there I lay in my mother's bed. I remember the conversation so vividly. He was asking her for sex.

She replied, "I'm on my cycle," and he replied, "So what!"

I remember thinking, *How nasty!* Since I was so young, I didn't know what part was nastier: them having sex or the period. I continued to lie still since she obviously didn't want to have sex with him as she gave yet another true excuse. "Armetria is right here, though," and again, he replied, "So what!"

They lay in that bed and had sex right while I was in the bed with them. I thought after all my mother had done to me, from abusing me, cursing me out, beating me black and blue, terrorizing me with tactics of fear, and smoking crack in my presence, this really took the cake. I had begun a journey toward HATING her. At that point, I didn't completely hate her because I still loved her, but the seed of hatred had begun to germinate. My respect for her as a woman was seriously tarnished.

Just a couple years later, my mother would get another boyfriend named Bobby. He was another big-time drug dealer from Jamaica that lived in New York. I got along with him much better than her previous one.

One day, he left a loaded gun in my room. I walked in from school that day to find my mom and Bobby fighting. I never liked to see anyone hitting or beating on my mother, so I tried to help her by screaming, "Stop! Please stop! Get off of my mother please!" He didn't listen. She began bidding me to give her some pliers that were on the television in her room. After getting them for her, she was still not able to get him off of her as she tried to pry his ear off. While all of this was happening, one of her drug addict friends was sitting right there in the bedroom in a chair, watching as my mother was getting her butt whipped. He told me, "You stay out of it. They had a disagreement and they got to work it out." I didn't listen and ran to the kitchen. That was it! I got a knife and the rest was history! I begin to stab at this man that would not release my mother from his strong, manly grip. He let her loose then. Later on, I would be approached by his mafia or gang members who didn't believe a child could have done such damage. They questioned my mother, and then my mother was held back as they questioned me to ensure that what she said was true. After confirming that I had stabbed the man, I never saw them again. My mom continued to date him until he was hauled off to prison.

After that, my beautiful little sister would be born. I loved that baby with such a passion! I despised my mother for smoking crack the entire time she was pregnant with her. I felt a responsibility to protect her from all I had gone through. So, I did to the best of my little ability.

Life would continue with my mother again being inconsiderate. She would leave us in the house by ourselves or at times with strangers. I remember being held back in the first or second grade because I didn't go to school enough since I had to be in the house with my sister. The sad thing about that is I was a super smart little girl. In pre-K, I was reading from third-grade books. What potential lost!

I remember always allowing my mother to slide without holding her accountable for anything, but I grew up blaming her for everything! Every failure in my life was always linked to her or my father. I blamed them for my choice of the wrong man, not knowing how to treat the right one, dropping out of high school, going through a divorce, and even making my own wrong parental choices. I was mostly BITTER with my mother. So, deep beyond the surface I couldn't stand her, but always honored her by not being disrespectful.

I remember as clear as day the Lord revealing to me WHY I kept slipping in my walk with Him and through life. It was because I was in bondage! I was a prisoner in an invisible jail that no one knew was my home. I was tormented in that place. It created more self-hatred and such attractions of negativity in my life. The more I thought I was getting back at her by secretly hating her, the thicker the walls had become in my prison and the further I was separated from the only thing I had to count on, GOD. I had again started to verbally express that I had forgiven her, and all the same, the Lord would bring me right back to the place to see the condition of my heart. My heart was far from the words I spoke from my mouth. I was not meek in my forgiveness towards her. I was just waiting for her to say something or do something one more time, and I was going to flick off.

As an adult, I tolerated her when I had to. To me, she was just another crackhead that just happened to be my mother. I strongly disliked the feeling that I felt towards her. So, I decided to allow her to stay in my first apartment with me and my children. After going to work, I would return home to find her still asleep. I would fuss with her, saying, "You laid on the couch all day and did nothing?" She would just reply with "You are evil." I felt I was justified in giving her a hard time since she was in my house, eating my food, and sleeping all day, but my heart was still not loving, understanding, compassionate, or long-suffering with her. Later on that week after she left my home, I found my mother had gone through my closet and robbed me blind. She threw her dirty clothes in my closet and took my clothing that I worked hard for. I was pissed to the highest of pissedom. Is that a word? I guess if pissed had a kingdom it would be called pissedom.

As I moved through life, I began to gain a closer walk and relationship with God that was truly wonderful! She was out of sight and out of my mind. So, I felt I had no issues, but I still struggled terribly in my walk with the Lord. I was always stumbling and falling, finding myself in oodles of trouble. I couldn't seem to put my finger on why I couldn't break all the way through to another level in God. I now know that one reason was because I was shacking up and the other reason was because I thought I had forgiven my mother, but I hadn't. God had a creative way of showing me that I still had un-forgiveness in my heart. By the time I would be reunited with my mother again, I had moved into a condo, had a little car, a stable man (who is my husband today), and a great job in contract with DC government. I had gone from being homeless, divorced, on welfare, and in public housing to holding it down with my three children and experiencing somewhat of a normal life.

To embrace God and His creative way to starting me on the path of seeing my hidden agenda and hidden hatred for my mother, I received a phone call. My mother's boyfriend at the time called to warn me that my mother had been hauled off to jail, and here's the kicker...she was using my name. I thought, *Wait a minute! How is she able to do that? You mean to tell me that she has been arrested and is telling the police that she is me? I can't believe this!* (Thank God I am fully covered in the blood now!) I had a cursing spirit right at that moment. He began to explain to me this wasn't the first time she had done that to me, and he felt bad and needed to tell me. He pleaded and hoped I wasn't upset with him. I quickly ended the call by telling him, "My war is not with you."

Every emotion known to man came crashing down on my heart and mind like a tsunami. My emotions were out of control! All the memories of what my mother had ever done came back to the surface as it shook my life like an earthquake. All the things I said with my lips that I had forgiven her for and the relationship I thought I had with God was being questioned. Not only did I realize I had not forgiven her, but it was clearly and painfully obvious that I couldn't trust God enough to step back and allow Him to fight this battle or at least tell me how to. My house appeared to be built shabbily on sand instead of the rock.

My boyfriend at the time (who is now my beloved husband) attempted to calm me down. I began to scream in anger, tears, and frustration, expressing that I hated her and didn't want her in my life. What if I had gotten pulled over for something and the boys were with me? She didn't care about anyone or anything but herself. I hated her, and whatever I needed to do to clear my name and put her under the jail, I was willing to do. I was sick of her, just sick and tired. *Why does she run in and out of my life and bring all this drama?*

My husband asked me to remain calm and just call the police station to clear my name. I literally couldn't even comprehend what advice he was offering. All I could think about was how I wanted to open up a can of whip a** on her. Thank God I'm saved now! In my favor, my mother had gotten busted and the police had figured out that she wasn't Armetria Knight, but instead, she was the tall, light-skinned, green-eyed, straight-haired bandit.

After spending a week or two in jail, the collect calls and letters started flowing in. Her lawyer told her if she could get me to do something (don't remember what it was) and pay her bail, she could get out. With not an ounce of emotion towards this lady, I replied, "Well, I can't help you. Perhaps that's where you need to be to get yourself together and get into rehab." She assured me, "If you don't help me, I am going to kill myself. I'm telling you and it will be on you." I told her, "I will just have to take that risk. Talk to you later." Mind you, before all of this, I said I had forgiven her, would pray for her, and had lived for a year or two thinking I had forgiven her.

Until this happened, God showed me just what I was working with: an unforgiving, bitter, hidden hatred in my heart for my mother. My mother started to write me letters two to three times per week, and they were packed with scriptures. She spoke with a lot of sense. I was shocked actually. I started to feel sorry for her, and again, I said out of my mouth and truly thought in my heart that I'd forgiven her.

When my mother was finally released from prison, none of her other children wanted to support her. So, my husband and I did. We even sat in meetings with her at the Salvation Army. She and I seemed to be creating the perfect bond. We went out together, and at times, we even included my grandmother. We all took pictures during that season. Things seemed to be looking up. I really felt like all was good and I had forgiven her, but deep in my heart, I was always waiting for her to apologize for what she had done and allowed to happen to me.

My mother got a job and seemed really consistent with turning her life around. Oh my, how proud I was! She worked at a restaurant right down the street from my job, and I would go with some of my co-workers so she could cook for us. Man, the food was really good. I had even started allowing the children to visit with her and form a relationship. Things seemed to be PERFECT. I was finally getting the mom that I missed through the years. The mom that missed all of the mother-daughter tea parties at school, performances, and the list goes on and on. We were inseparable; I was loving her, longing for her.

One day, I had gone to her house after work to check on her because I didn't hear from her that day. The place where she worked had started to lay off employees, and she was one of them to be laid off. When I went by her house, some of the drug dealers that stood outside stared at me. They knew me from coming around and seemed to know that I wasn't at all fond of them. She had once introduced me to one of them, who I think had a little crush on me. I think we all know I would never go that route. Besides, I had a mighty good man at home.

Let's call the drug dealer with the crush Q. Q looked at me strangely as I approached my mother's doorpost. My feet that usually felt so light to run and see her somehow felt heavy as I got closer to her apartment door. Everyone stood around, literally, and stared at me enter as if the entire neighborhood was in mourning. I knocked and knocked at her door, but no one answered. After my knuckles and hand became sore, I made my way back out to the sad block and approached Q.

"Q, have you seen my mother?" I asked, and he replied, "Yeah, she's in there."

He went in and knocked harder than I ever could, and then left as she scrambled to open the door. Before opening it, I could hear the difference in her voice, and my heart fell from my chest to my feet. I felt an emptiness that I'd never felt before. I thought I was going to throw-up. She opened the door, and immediately, I looked into her eyes and interrogated her like I was trying to solve a murder.

I said, "I had been knocking for a while. What were you doing?" She replied, stuttering and inconsistent with tone and word, "I was sleep. I'm just sleepy." All of the dark memories of her smoking crack in my presence when I was young overtook my mind, will, and emotion. I hated her all over again. I started to go off!

I said, "Momma, are you HIGH?" She began to stutter. "Armetria, please, I'm resting." I begged her, "Mommy, tell me the truth. Are you high?" She began to tell me, "I just smoked a little weed, that's all. That doesn't even get me high."

All the time, she still had not let me in the door. I marched up those steps to again approach Q and the crew to give them a piece of my mind. I walked up to him cussing out of control. "Which one of you MOTHER- (you know what) sold my mother drugs?" The tears rolled down my face uncontrollably. I was completely and thoroughly hurt down to my very soul. Eyeliner and makeup mixed with what seemed to be tears of acid burned my eyes as the realization of what my mother had done burned my heart. My knees buckled, and as I began to feel weak and sick, I grabbed my tummy. My father had warned me that this would happen, but I had gotten angry with him because I felt he was just poking fun at my mom.

Reality set in, and as much as I don't want to say it, my dad was right. The court placed her in rehab. She didn't go because she wanted to be set free; she went because she had to.

Q began to explain, "You know I was all for Angie being clean. I was proud of her. She would come out here begging us, but nobody would serve her 'cause we knew you were coming around with the kids and she was trying to pull it together. I promise you that we didn't do it." I replied, "Well, somebody sold it to her or gave it to her. Who was it?" He informed me that it was her next-door neighbor. I asked, "Is he in there now?" Q replied, "Yeah, but don't try to fight him or nothing 'cause he got that monkey real strong on his back." I was like, "What? He has a monkey?" With a half smile, Q responded, "Naw, he got AIDS real bad."

I still proceeded to knock on his door and he answered. This man looked like hell on wheels. I just turned and walked away back to my mother's apartment where my kids' bikes were. I busted through the door and said, "Give me my kids stuff before you go and sell it. I knew you weren't going to do right. I knew you would fail." She began to explain, "I don't need this, Armetria. I made a mistake. I'm sorry."

I grabbed my kids' stuff, packed it in my car, and left. I cried all the way home. I was so paralyzed with pain that I couldn't even form a word in prayer. I felt let down. Again, I asked myself, "Why is it that every time I let her into my life she hurts me?"

Reflections

In this chapter, I dealt with a lot of issues, and they were all linked to a strong, overbearing force called UNFORGIVENESS.

First of all, I didn't understand forgiveness, which is one of the reasons I would fail in life over and over. I was a prisoner in my own personal tormenting chamber. I hated out loud, and then when things were calm because I thought and said I had forgiven, I hated in secret. I dealt with a lot. My flesh would say my mother didn't deserve forgiveness, but God's truth says she does.

I had begun to realize I was no different than my mother in my relationship with God. I would love Him and then run out with the enemy and hurt Him. No, I wasn't on drugs and didn't do the things she did, but my disobedience towards God was just like a drug. I seemed to do what I wanted to do. Thus, hurting God the way my mother hurt me. God is forgiving and loving in his approach to correction with me. I often wondered why I struggled in my relationship with God. Then I asked Him, "Why can't I remain stable in You and do the right thing?" My mother would always enter my life and wreak some kind of havoc at that very point. Let me put this in prospective. God loves us so much that He wouldn't withhold any good thing from us. Shining a light of illumination on me, naked and barren in the midst of the wilderness, God showed me how my mouth would say one thing, but when confronted with an emotional blow from my mom, I did another.

This was the KEY to my hang-ups in relationship with God. Most likely, when one is bitten by a venomous snake, another person must come and create a sharp incision to the bite. This would allow an outlet for the venom to pour out of the wound. Not until that painful incision is made does the venom have another place to go other than your vital organs and cause death. Every painful encounter with my mother was God's incision in my wound to free me from a life-threatening poison.

The same holds true with a devastating blow to the emotions. It's like a fatal bite from a seriously poisonous snake. The only way to save your life is to confront any un-forgiveness or bitterness you may be harboring. Look deep and ask yourself the key questions. Do I always expect this person to apologize for what they have done? Do I keep repeating that I have forgiven them and I wish them no harm? This could be an indicator that you are trying to convince yourself that you have forgiven, but you haven't forgiven at all.

Here's a list of possible signs that un-forgiveness is lacking in your life:
- Memory of the hurt surfacing frequently
- Desire to punish the person or make him or her pay
- Feelings of bitterness
- Anger with God
- Chronic irritability or negativity
- Disturbed sleep
- Positive life goals interrupted by negative thoughts
- Signs of traumatic stress (flashbacks, anxiety, disturbing dreams, etc.)
- Looking for an apology from that person

If you feel there is any inkling or indication that you could be harboring resentment, bitterness, and un-forgiveness, I pray that the Lord will use me right now as a knife to create the incision to allow the poison to flow freely away from your vital organs. The only possible way to release the poison is to get it out of your head and your heart, and onto some paper. My friend, this is a powerful journey we are on. However, I promise if you continue the walk, you will be destined to arrive at a place of peace with God, yourself, and others.

Make a list of some people, places, and things that may have caused you hurt that you have never dealt with. Now ask yourself: Is being at peace with God worth me forgiving this? Is being free from this pain and agony worth me releasing this? Is loving myself totally and purely worth me forgiving this? We must remember forgiveness is a choice, not an option!

Healing Balm for the Soul

Be kind and compassionate to one another, forgiving each other, just as in Christ God forgave you.

Ephesians 4:32

For if you forgive men when they sin against you, your heavenly Father will also forgive you. But if you do not forgive men their sins, your Father will not forgive your sins.

Matthew 6:14-15

Beloved, never avenge yourselves, but leave the way open for [God's] wrath; for it is written vengeance is Mine. I will repay (require), says the Lord.

Romans 12:19

A Love Letter to You

Beloved,

    Although it may seem as if you lose out by forgiving, how awesome is it that our dynamic heavenly Father says we gain so much. We gain forgiveness from Him when we free ourselves to forgive others. Notice that God wants to fight your battles. He simply wants you to live in the freedom that He has your back. So, go ahead and love on yourself by constantly reminding yourself that God has not forgotten anything that has been done to or against you. He loves you so much that He wants you to release it so that HE may take on your enemies. You are so loved that the Father of all creation will go to bat on your behalf. Enjoy your freedom in having a loving and forgiving heart because you look just like your Father. (Genesis 1:27)

Lovingly,
Armetria

A JOURNEY TO SELF LOVE

THE TUG OF WAR OF FORGIVING ME

Chapter 8

ARMETRIA M. CHARLES

The Tug of War in Forgiving Me

At the tender age of sixteen years old, my temple would become a home to a fetus that I knew nothing about nor understood how precious it was.

I was pregnant! I remember the day I found out and how all kinds of emotions flew through my body as I sat in Children's Hospital. I couldn't stop vomiting, and everyone thought I had a flu or virus. Little did they know that I was between six to twelve weeks pregnant.

When the doctor finally announced to me and a friend of the family my diagnosis, a flood of adrenaline traveled through me at warp speed. Every question known to man crowded my mind. *Is it possible to keep it? Is it a girl or a boy? Will I be a good mom? My goodness, what on earth am I asking myself? My father is going to kill me, and that's not a question.*

I was depressed and felt tormented at home. I had to be extra careful walking around the house and guarded, so as to not let any of my aunts or my grandmother get a good look at me. I didn't want to risk that some of those old wives' tales and super human signs had shown up on me.

I was scared to death and would sit in class staring into space while contemplating my demise. I had heard of abortion, which seemed to be my only option at the time, because if my dad found out, he was going to kill me. That was the record that played over and over in my head. I needed a rescue mission and I needed one quickly. I didn't want to be a mom just yet; I didn't want to be a huge disappointment to my father and the rest of the family. I suffered inwardly and felt terrible about the thoughts that plagued me. I told the father of the child that I couldn't have the baby and that we must figure something out because my dad would seriously kill me...and him too, for that matter. He didn't want me to have an abortion, but with the fear that overtook me, I felt I had no other option.

Soon enough, my school counselors and the principle found out and helped me keep it a secret from my family. They even scheduled the appointment for my abortion. I had no clue mentally what I was setting myself up for. I went to Planned Parenthood under the direction of my school and was a part of the MURDER of my baby boy or girl. I can never forget the feelings that tormented me. I was counseled by the Planned Parenthood abortion counselor, but she never mentioned anything about the torment, mental agony, and stress that I'd face after the procedure.

After experiencing such a horrific procedure, I was as sick as a cancer patient. I had fluid gushing out of both ends. Something seriously wrong could have happened and my parents wouldn't have known crap. After a day or so, I felt relieved physically, but mentally, I was haunted and tormented by the spirit of murder. I did everything I could to ignore it, justify it, and get over it, but it continued to plague me.

I grew up making more and more bad decisions. You name it and I did it. Sleeping around with different guys, lying to get what I wanted, and disobeying my father to name a few. My juvenile record was horrible. I was always getting arrested for something, from shoplifting, fighting, and even driving without a license. It didn't take me long to realize that jail was not the place for me. So, I got my act together and started doing other things that didn't really affect anyone or anything directly except me.

I would always find really great boyfriends that were into me and would have probably given me the world, but I would mistreat them for no reason. I would do and say hurtful things to people just because I didn't care. I was what some would call "wishy washy" and I didn't care. I ended up being forced into a marriage at the age of eighteen by my ex-husband's mother who held an office in the church. Marrying her son was to protect her family's image. I hated every day spent in that marriage. It made me wish I had never gotten pregnant again at seventeen and left my grandmother's house. I was afraid my dad would find out about the pregnancy and would want me to abort the baby. By then, I had begun modeling, and my career was starting to take off. He said a baby would slow me down. He told me that I knew what I had to do and proceeded to give me some money. I knew one thing for sure, I wasn't having another abortion. I told him I was not going to do it! He said, "So you're going to let some baby come and mess your whole life up?" I replied, "Yes." He was very angry and said, "Well, you had better find you somewhere else to live."

I took him seriously and did just that. I quickly felt regret about leaving. Leaving pushed me into the deadly trap of unwanted marriage with the father of my unborn baby. Once I made the decision to marry him, I hated him and myself. It was like hell on earth living and being with him and his mother. I was imprisoned due to the both of them. The decisions I made had landed me there.

Choosing to marry this man led me into a place of continuous emotional, verbal, and sometimes physical abuse. I didn't know the Word of God for myself, so his mother would make sure she kept me in bondage by saying, "A piece of man is better than no man." She always had this dumb smirk on her face that seemed to say, "You know I got you now." She would remind me that if I ever left her son and married someone else, my marriage would be adulterous and God would not honor it.

So many times I would cry and fall into spells of deep depression. She had a heavy stronghold of witchcraft (manipulation) over me, and worse, I believed her. I felt there was no way out of the torment of staying in her unfinished basement. There was wet clothing everywhere (from everyone washing their clothes) hanging over my head. I tried many times to kill myself. They knew that basement was a horrible place to stay. Even my husband at the time chose to stay upstairs where it was warm and finished. I went through hell in that place. I was even attending church with the mom, which was a requirement except for her son. He was the only one that was not forced to go. I am actually glad I went, because I learned a lot about how amazing God is. Unfortunately, I didn't learn enough to release me from the bondage that was inflicted upon me by my mother-in-law.

After a while, I got a job, began making my own money, and prepared myself to leave someday. I had started an adulterous affair with a man at the job. I didn't feel an ounce of remorse and just hated my situation.

The mental and spiritual abuse was overbearing. One night, I asked permission (yes, I said asked permission) to go and see my father. I missed my dad so much, but my husband hated my dad. He wanted me to love him on the same level as my continued love for my father. He would always make reference to when my dad did something how I would be quick to throw him back on a pedestal, and he felt he was the one who did everything for me.

I had planned to escape that night. I begged, "I saw my dad's truck as we were coming in from church. May I go to see my dad please?" He replied, "For what? That West Nile virus is out." So, I replied, "Well, you keep the baby and I'll be back in a few."

He continued to fuss, while I begged all the more to see my daddy. Finally, he released me to go. He said, "You got twenty minutes, and I mean it!"

I didn't care what he was saying. I was so glad he said I could go. I missed my dad and our already shattered relationship had crumbled more and more. I wanted to protect the fragments, if that's what it took. My grandmother's house was literally around the corner, so I took off running to catch my daddy before he left. Low and behold, he was still at grandma's house. I came and paid respects to my grandmother, and then went right into the other room where my dad and I could talk in private.

I had begun to show signs of wanting out of what I had gotten myself into. I told him in a weak and timid voice, "Dad, I think I made a mistake." It wasn't strong enough to convince him. Therefore, he didn't take me seriously. He got on the phone and started having a conversation with someone else. Then, phone calls began to come in on my grandmother's line. "Metra, your husband is on the phone," she yelled out to me. When I picked up, it was him saying my time was up. I began to plead, "But I just got here. I've only been here about ten minutes." At least that's all it felt like to me. He started to yell that I needed to get home. Perhaps he could sense in his spirit that Armetria wanted out of that hellhole called home and that demonic stronghold called a marriage.

I fell at the edge of the bed at my father's feet and began to weep in hopes that he would feel my pain. I mean, the tears were really coming down. The daughter's strong voice that he once knew to be a singer, actress, and model had been diminished to barely a whisper, as I looked up to see that my father had fallen asleep. I silently cried, "Daddy, please help me. I've made a huge mistake and I'm sorry."

My grandmother began to yell again. "Armetria!" Whenever she said my full first name, she meant business. "Armetria, this boy say the baby's behind is bleeding!" I replied, "WHAT? His behind is bleeding?" She took her hand and covered the phone so my husband couldn't hear her, then said to me, "He said he needs you to tell him where the insurance card is. He got to take him to the hospital because his butt is bleeding." I took the phone to hear that he was telling the biggest lie ever. I said to him, "I will be there in about five minutes." He began yelling, "You need to come now and I mean now!" I suppose my grandmother could hear the yelling and understood that he wanted me home because she said to me, "You a married woman now, baby, so you need to go so it won't be any trouble." I cried as I went to the room to tell my sleeping daddy goodbye.

I left, walked around the corner, and knocked on the door. Yes, I said knocked because they never gave me a key even though I lived there. The baby was crying while my husband's mother and sister were sitting in the living room.

When I came in the door, he came rushing towards me. "Didn't I tell you to hurry up home?" He grabbed my throat, twisted my arm up behind my back, threw me outside on the porch, and screamed, "GO BACK WITH YOUR CRACKHEAD (you know what) FATHER"! I got up off the ground and began banging on the door, screaming with the little voice I had left from being choked and thrown out by my throat. I was sure that since his mother and sister were sitting there that they would rescue me and open the door. I thought maybe they would play mediators, but it never happened. I banged and screamed in a raspy, shaky voice, "Give me my baby!"

At this point, neither his family nor mine had extended a single hand to help me. I felt worthless, scared, and outraged all at the same time. Being forced to detach from my newborn baby boy was horrifying! I mustered up the strength to run back around the corner to my grandmother's home, crying and extremely emotional. I ran up the stairs, and my father was awakened abruptly by my painstaking cries.

He hopped up yelling, "Did that nigga put his hands on you?"

I was so emotional and disoriented that I don't remember how I responded. Whatever my response was, my dad was on a mission to take him out. My grandmother immediately intercepted the ball of fury and warned him to allow me to handle it properly. She handed me the telephone and encouraged me to get the police involved.

I was really afraid then. Although I had been hurt by this man and his family, I was still very emotional and didn't want to get him into trouble. I did as my grandmother suggested, though, and while crying, I called and reported everything to the police.

Once the police came, all I could get out was, "I want my baby! They have my baby!" The officer explained to my father and grandmother that they would take me to get my baby and my belongings. We arrived at the door, and when the police began knocking loudly, my mother-in-law opened the door. They asked her if he was there in the house, and she replied, "No, he has gone out searching for her, his wife." They then asked to come in and she hesitantly allowed us access. They began to inquire about my son and she passed him along to me. I then expressed to the police that I needed clothing and my belongings. They asked me where they were, and I pointed to the basement where I once lived. They had me show them to the dungeon, the place where all of my torment had began as a young adult. As usual, my mother-in-law lied through her teeth in a huge effort to protect her abusive son. He was right there hiding out in the basement as I had expected he would be.

    They arrested him immediately, while his mother stood there reminding me of how another one of her sons would be in jail behind a woman. She also began to tell me how she wanted me out of her house. Did she really believe I wanted to be there with her after all of that? I think not! I left and stayed with my grandmother for a few days, then at my cousin's place for another week or so, and then back to my grandmother's home again. Everyone seemed to be so incredibly supportive in my family, for a little while.

    I will never forget. It was around Christmas time and I heard my grandmother speaking with my aunt. I suppose my aunt was asking if she was going to allow me to come back home, and I heard my grandmother reply, "No, she can't come back here. I don't know where she's going, but you know family is coming up this year. So, they are going to have to go somewhere." That hurt me to the core of my soul. I began calling homeless shelters to find a place for me and my little baby to stay. There was nowhere. It seemed so hard and I had been beaten down so much. I didn't even come right out and tell my dad. I think I expected him to read my mind. Little did he know I had no place to go.

    There was this guy who liked me a great deal, and when I ran out of every resource for places to stay, I allowed an adulterous relationship with him to have a place. He was very nice and treated me well, but I didn't want to be with anyone. I simply wanted a place to call home.

    During that period, I found a job and was determined to make it, but as it turned out, I failed. I began working for a hotel and got childcare for my baby boy where I was paying $160.00 per week, so I worked overtime like crazy. I left early and wouldn't see my baby boy until late in the evening. It wasn't long before my husband began calling my job to ask me to drop the charges and say that I was lying about him choking me and throwing me out the door. I couldn't extend that favor to him because I wasn't lying. I was telling the truth. I told him I would drop the charges, though. As a result of having to take off so much and being late because of court appearances, I lost my job. I was deeply crushed because I thought the money from the job would help to build my getaway fund that was part of my exit plan. I found another place to stay since I hated living with another man just for shelter when he really loved me. Because I wasn't able to return those feelings of love, I felt horrible!

I went back and tried to help my husband, the very person that continued to hurt me. I went to court for him in an effort to show the judge that we were together and happy so he could be considered to be released from the charges. At the time, I think they were only for probation. He begged me to come and stand in support. With no money and no place to go, I went. He went into the courtroom, got his answer from the judge, and snuck out of the courthouse without me even knowing it.

The baby and I had been sitting there for hours with no signs of his father. I continued to wait until the lawyer came out and asked me why I was still there. I told him I was waiting for my husband, to which he replied, "He has been gone for over two hours now."

I burst into tears because I had no money, no diapers, and no food or milk for the baby. He left me stranded, literally stranded! When I squeezed the bottom of my son's diaper, I knew if he urinated one more time, the diaper would fall apart. The lawyer asked me if there was someone to pick me up and I told him the truth. "No, sir, there's no one." I continued crying as he reached into his pocket and pulled out all the money he could find it. It was enough to get a bite to eat for me and my son. I also made a few phone calls, including one to my dad's current girlfriend who got her friend to come and give me a ride. I went back to the dungeon because although he had left me high and dry, it was Friday and his weekend to keep the baby. After leaving there, I went and stayed with a girlfriend, as I was always from pillar to post.

One weekend, when going to drop my son off to his father, I waited there with his mother. My husband never showed up. His mother encouraged me to wait around a few minutes more when suddenly, a collect call came in stating that he had been arrested. His mother was nervous and both of us were wondering what had happened.

In an attempt to get help for my son's father, I called an old Law & Society teacher that I knew who was still a head lawyer at PDS (Public Defender Services) to tell him a story that wasn't even true. I expressed that he had been wrongfully arrested and set up by some undercover cops. My resource looked his case up and informed me that he had lied to me and actually sold drugs to an undercover officer. Wow, what a blow! I should have known he couldn't be trusted to tell me the truth, even with the reason he was arrested. I wasn't sure what to do at that point because I was still homeless, and although I had never wanted to be there again, it was all I knew in my condition of low self-worth.

I ended up taking the baby and staying somewhere that weekend. We moved around to so many places that I can't even remember where we stayed. After a few weeks, I took my son to visit his grandmother, and when I was preparing to leave, my husband called and wanted to speak with me. He expressed that he wanted to work things out, and that he had found God and didn't want me and his son running the streets. I enjoyed having freedom, but I didn't like not having a steady place to go and having to replace clothing for me and my son due to moving around a lot. I melted hearing him talk like that for the very first time. I was amazed and dazzled that perhaps this forced marriage could somehow turn out to be something good.

I moved back in, cutting off all other relationships outside of our marriage. The guy who had provided shelter, food, and other things was incredibly disappointed and hurt when I cut him completely off. He begged me not to go back. He warned me that my husband was telling great lies and would never treat me right. I shut him out and up! I was back in the dungeon again, but things seemed great for a moment.

My husband came home from jail and seemed to be God's gift to me.

It wasn't long before we would be pregnant with our second child, and again, our marriage was hell on wheels. I was in and out again, staying with anyone who would allow me to stay with them. Then I would come back again, until finally I got sick and tired of being just that…sick and tired. I remember my father telling me, "I will bail you out just once, but if you go back, that's it. You will have to figure things out on your own." Somehow in the midst of all that drama, I forgot about my bailout plan. I began working again and even tried to work things out with my husband over and over again.

I started to realize that he would never move us out of his mother's house. It was like I was married to her and suffered a lot of emotional abuse from her in addition to the abuse from my husband. She had a way of working overtime to make me feel small. One day, I called the crisis hotline because I was ready to leave. I hated that place since no one had accepted my second son and treated my baby like crap. I ended up talking to a social worker from the crisis hotline that encouraged me to try and work on my marriage. So, that's what I did. At that time, I still didn't have a job. The social worker made every effort to try to find a place for our family. I believe he could see that the interference from my mother-in-law placed great strain on the marriage. I did everything I was asked to do to make it work, yet nothing worked. Every apartment we tried to lease together would fail. No one was willing to help us as a couple. One property manager spoke with me privately and said, "I would take you and those kids in, but I can't accept your husband." As crazy as that sounds, imagine how I felt. When nothing would work for us and people were willing to take me with no job and leave him out with a job, that spoke volumes to me that we weren't suppose to be together.

Things started to get more and more heated in the home. Adhering to the counsel of the social worker, I accepted a night job. I worked hard every night and started to create my exit strategy. One day, a light went off in my head that reminded me of my father's bailout strategy. I called and told him I needed to find an apartment that I could afford, and that the social worker would help me purchase furniture and everything. For the first time, I spoke up and my father moved. He saved my life by pulling strings with a friend that found an affordable place for me to stay. I didn't say a word about my plan to leave. On the day I got the call from the lady saying I could move in, I called my father and told him to gather some men while my husband and his mother were at work. My father moved quickly as he flew in like a knight in shining armor and rescued me. When he had finally seen the dungeon for the first time, he cried and said, "I had no idea you had to live like this. They kept you in a dungeon!"

I then moved into my own place, where I would make mistake after mistake. I enjoyed my reckless life; I didn't care. I didn't believe God could ever forgive me for divorce or any of the other things I had done. I remembered my ex-husband's mother's words ringing in my ear: "If you leave or divorce my son, God will never honor you marrying another man." As a result of being haunted by those words, I contemplated suicide. I mean, no one wants God to be angry with them. I wanted a relationship with God, but could never get close to having one because I believed every word my mother-in-law had spoken to me. I actually said out of my mouth, "God, if you can't forgive me for a mistake I made in my youth, I want nothing to do with you."

It wasn't long before I experienced a nervous breakdown and began to lose my mind. I had shaved my head bald with a razor! All of my so-called friends had turned against me in one day. I had never been in such a dark place in my life. People were trying to get me evicted from my apartment, and child protection services were called with false reports made against me. My children were placed in their father's custody while I was investigated. During that lonely time, I was forced to the lowest and most pivotal point in my life, on my knees. I screamed out to God nothing more than, "HELP ME! PLEASE HELP ME!"

For some strange reason, the only thing I could find was the Yellow Pages. I began flipping through the pages and found a prayer hotline called the Upper Room. I called and poured out to that woman who I didn't know and who would be a prayer partner with me. She ministered to me and then asked me something really enlightening. "Did God put you and this man together or his mother?"

As I began to pick up the pieces and find God for myself and talk to Him, He quickly revealed to me that I had not come to Him. I was angry with Him for something that someone else had said to me. My marriage was not a marriage at all, but instead, it was a counterfeit and manipulative method that was used to control me. I remember when God set me free. After gaining access to the Father myself, I found that He was very loving and kind. He was forgiving and not like people.

I got my children back because they couldn't prove nor find anything that supported the lie that I was a negligent parent. The property manager, who was being urged to put me out, gave me a larger, much better apartment, and later even created resources for me to get a townhome. It was a process towards restoration to rise above all that I had brought down on myself.

Reflections

Wow, what a chapter! I dealt with such condemnation that led to more condemnation that led to me not wanting a relationship with God. Now that was heavy! Unforgiveness is a major hindrance when dealing with ourselves. I had never received God's full forgiveness when I got the abortion, divorce, cursed my relationship with God, and did things that I was ashamed of. I continuously found myself asking Him to forgive me over and over again because I was searching for a feeling of being forgiven. The piece I was missing was forgiveness is not a feeling. When you've prayed and asked God to forgive you. it is what it is. YOU ARE FORGIVEN! God has simply said NOT GUILTY!

It was incredibly hard for me to break the mindset that somehow it was too good to be true that just by asking and having a change of heart in regards to my wrongdoing, I was forgiven. When I rehearsed the things that God had forgiven me for, yet had not forgiven myself, I would find myself repeating the same sinful behaviors. That wasn't the first abortion I had and it certainly wasn't the last. I had two of them, and it probably would have continued if I had not forgiven me. Forgiving yourself simply means you believe God over everything anyone else could be saying against you or whatever you could be saying against yourself. There will be many reminders of our hurtful, sinful past, but you must hold fast to the WORD of God that says old things are passed away. You're a brand-new creature.

We are so conditioned to man and his ways that when God shows us a more loving and sincere way, it's hard for us to accept and believe. Stop yourself right now and reflect on those thoughts, actions, or words that you may be holding against yourself. Simply free yourself from the guilt and shame of your past by receiving God's gift of forgiveness. It's simply one prayer away!

Healing Balm for the Soul

"Bless the Lord, O my soul, and forget not all his benefits, who forgives all (not some of) your iniquity, who heals all your diseases."

Psalms 103:1-3 (emphasis added)

"Blessed is the man whose sin the Lord does not count against him and in whose spirit is no deceit. When I kept silent, my bones wasted away through my groaning all day long. For day and night your hand (of judgment) was heavy upon me; my strength was sapped as in the heat of summer. Then I acknowledged my sin to you and did not cover up my iniquity. I said, "I will confess my transgressions to the Lord"-- and you forgave the guilt of my sin."

Psalm 32:1-5 (emphasis added)

"I write to you, dear children, because your sins have been forgiven on account of his name."

1 John 2:12

A Love Letter to You

Beloved,

You are so loved and incredibly safe in His arms. Know that God gets no glory out of you feeling condemned, forsaken, shameful, or hurt. He wants you fulfilled, forgiven, and free. He wants you to come boldly to the throne of grace to obtain mercy because He wants you to have full confidence that your Father is a loving father who forgives and forgets. He's crazy about you! Jesus was given because God already knew that you would do what you've done. He bore your sins in his very own body. You have been released; your debts have been paid. Ain't nobody mad but the devil! Remember, when the enemy comes trying to remind you of your past, remind him of his future. (Revelation 20:10)

Lovingly,
Armetria

A JOURNEY TO SELF LOVE

Picking Up The Pieces

Chapter 9

ARMETRIA M. CHARLES

Picking up the Pieces

I remember when I decided to lay it all down and live for the Lord. I was happy and in love with God. I thought nothing would ever go wrong. I would begin to live my life carefree now that I was a brand-new creature and brand-new woman. No one told me it was a process. Looking back over my life, I thought of everything I had gone through as stumbling blocks. I felt I was a victim of circumstance and dealt a bad hand in life. Little did I know that all of these things would work together for the best! Everything — the good, bad, and indifferent — was part of the awesome design of me. I remember making mistakes within my walk with God, and I would beat myself up about it for days. It would often leave me so broken and bound that I would fall deeper into wrongdoings and sin.

As you have read, I've faced some serious hardships, but those hardships are nothing like the glory I am experiencing right now, and even the glory to come. Life can come at us hard, but what I've learned is that no matter what we've faced, we must understand it's all part of the divine purpose that has already existed within us from the very beginning. I'm a prime example of that.

I think back to being afraid of the closet that God tells us is a room for prayer and intimacy with Him, and how it was used as a tool of torture and fear for me. The connected dot, there was the enemy who knew I would have a gift to intercede on behalf of countless others. I thank you, Lord, for deliverance and total healing. I look back on how I felt when I didn't have anything to eat and my tummy would rumble. Now I can have compassion for the people and children in other countries and even my own that are impoverished and need something to eat. It was so I can know firsthand what it felt like to be without food and then be a resource to provide food for others.

I am reminded of a shattered life as I look back on all of the broken glass of my past. I remember the day I met my savior, and He helped me pick up the pieces that I thought carried no value. He gave me hope, a promise, and a stain that was from his mighty transforming blood. From that I created a mosaic-stained glass masterpiece. Oddly, I was doing some research and found out that mosaic pieces are very prevalent in the holy land.

I connected the dots to being molested and abused terribly with the fact that I am a resilient woman through Christ, my king, and a vessel of hope and promise for countless others who have suffered by the hand of some poor soul that is tortured. God has raised me up to be a voice for the voices that have been quieted by little family secrets and abuse. The dots are connected from a crazy and terrible looking past to a great and rewarding present and future. I didn't understand why I had gone through it at the time, but I understand it now. Many didn't even realize the part they played; a major part in the greatness that would spring forth through Christ in me.

I am grateful for my past as I anticipate my future. I shall run and not faint! All I know is, if I had never experienced darkness, I wouldn't have known what it was to experience the light. If I had never been broken, I wouldn't know what it was like to be restored. If I had never been forsaken, I wouldn't know what it was like to be received into the beloved. Glory, I feel my help coming now! If I had never experienced abandonment from my parents, I wouldn't know what it was like to experience ALMIGHTY GOD! If I was never raped, used, and abused, I wouldn't know what it was like to be loved, cherished, respected, and adored. If I had never experienced any knucklehead counterfeit lovers, I wouldn't have known or come to respect true love in my husband.

See, I have connected the dots. Although the dots of my past are dark and dreary, they connect to a present and a future that no one can fully understand and the enemy can EVER touch. I have been healed, set free, and delivered, and for that, God, I live for you. With all my broken pieces and the stain you have provided, I add the final glass and am now considered "The Master's Piece."

Reflections

Count it all joy! You have gone through some serious trials in your life and guess what? Someone who has gone through something similar didn't make it. You are a survivor, you are a champion, you are a designer's original, and you are the master's piece! Let me break that down.

If you took one of your favorite garments and flipped it inside out, it wouldn't look so great. You couldn't wear it looking like that. It looks unfinished; it looks undone. Strings are probably hanging, and you can see bold stitching in the fabric. You can witness where there have been cuts, grooves, and multiple stitching. Let me tell you, it was all a part of the plan. The work happens on the inside of the garment in the process of its past, and it's a private battle. Nobody knows the struggle or whether or not the garment was handled with care. All we know is at the end of production we have been blessed with a beautiful garment that is easy on the eyes and great to your designer taste. Every stitch, cut, dye, and awkward tracing was all part in creating the beautiful finished product of your favorite garment. So, everything that you have struggled and battled with internally was a private stitching process that connected the dots to public fashion highly sought after. Remember, there is value in the valley, and as my dad once told me, you have to embrace the valley before you can get to the mountain.

Your past plays a significant part in creating a DYNAMIC future and a more equipped YOU. Hang in there. You are privately being stitched, cut, and formulated, but the awesomeness is the fruit therein that will be public for all to see. Don't be so hard on yourself when you fall and make a mistake while making your steps to Christ. Understand that growing in God is a lifetime process.

Healing Balm for the Soul

The end of a matter is better than its beginning, and patience is better than pride.

Ecclesiastes 7:8

For his anger is but for a moment, and his favor is for a lifetime. Weeping may tarry for the night, but joy comes with the morning.

Psalms 30:5

"For I know the plans I have for you," declares the LORD. "Plans to prosper you and not to harm you, plans to give you hope and a future.

Jeremiah 29:11

A Love Letter to You

Beloved,

Count it all joy that you have been set aside for greatness! God has always had great thoughts towards you and wonderful plans for you. Your past was simply a part of our divine purpose. God wants you to know He has never left your side and He never will. All of the things you have experienced all worked towards the greater good within you. Your beginning may have not been so great, but the word declares the end of a matter is better than the beginning. With that in mind, I am expecting great things to spring forth in you. God finds joy in your strength and you'll find great strength in God's joy. (Nehemiah 8:10)

Lovingly,
Armetria

A JOURNEY TO SELF LOVE

The WOW Factor
Chapter 10

ARMETRIA M. CHARLES

The Wow Factor

Throughout my journey in creating a stable and fabulous life, I had many tell me that I couldn't do it, that it wasn't worth the fight, that I would fail, and that I didn't have the education or the background. I know somebody who tried it and it didn't work for them. There were many that were simply afraid of sharing my visions and passions in becoming a writer, minister of the gospel, and life empowerment coach. In the past, when I would share certain dreams and aspirations with family and so-called friends, they would find some way to speak death upon them. It would shatter my dreams and any hope I had of starting a journey and making them come true. In life, I have had relationships with many haters, and their assignments were to stop my process and kill my journey. Those people came in the form of family members, close friends, naysayers, and simply voices from within. As we take a look back down memory lane, I think about those in my old high school who felt I was slow and not mature enough to handle the world. Also, there were those who rejected me and abandoned me, not understanding the greatness within me. To all of the folks who couldn't stand me, fought me, wouldn't help me, rejected me, slowed me down, cast me out, shut me up, abused me, and are still trying to stop me, I have one thing to say — W.O.W. (With Or Without You). I am moving forth in a life full of freedom, love, peace, and joy. I will be successful... I am successful, and I know I will soar high above the clouds.

I remember hearing teachers tell other students in my presence that the sky was the limit for them, clearly to be an indirect insult to me. That used to hurt, but now it doesn't because I have discovered that they were right. The sky is the limit for some; however, for me, it can't be the limit when there are footprints on the moon. I will climb higher and try harder to break every mode. It is very clear to me that people will try to stop you when you think differently and outside of the imaginary box that the average person lives in. They will try and break you based on what you do and don't have.

I was told I was dark and ugly with nappy hair but W.O.W that hasn't stopped me from becoming one of the most powerful women I know. I remember every time I would have an idea, a vision, or a dream, I was looked at like I was crazy or like I spoke an unknown language. I would be counted out because I didn't look popular or was not accepted because I came from a different background. W.O.W I made it! To every job that I applied for that literally laughed in my face, W.O.W, you were a part of my purpose in the process.

This chapter is not to bash anyone, but it is simply to encourage YOU to pursue your dreams no matter how crazy or farfetched they may seem to others. God has given us all visions as well as the ability to dream. Don't allow anyone to stop that within you. Not everyone will agree with your decision to shine. There will be people who feel you are destined to maintain a mediocre life. Well, I declare that you shall LIVE and not DIE! Your dream must go on! The ministry within you must be birthed; the fight in you must not be stopped. You have everything in you to win. You were born equipped to succeed and survive.

Reflections

Recognize who and whose you are. Others that can't come into agreement with you and your decision to fly or move past ordinary, simply tell them, W.O.W. (With Or Without them) you shall fly and be EXTRAORDINARY. Start to practice walking in your own destiny and not the path that was laid by others. Create your own path and follow it with all of your heart. Know that you can do all things through Christ who strengthens you.

Healing Balm for the Soul

"He who walks with wise men will be wise, but the companion of fools will be destroyed."

Proverbs 13:20

Stay away from fools, for you won't find knowledge there.

Proverbs 14:7

Don't be fooled by those who say such things, for "bad company corrupts good character."

1 Corinthians 15:33

A Love Letter to You

Beloved,

    We have completed this particular journey, and you have been filled with much encouragement and many wise words. If no one else tells you this, please believe me when I say I don't care what the shortcoming, the past situation, what your family and friends may think, or what the enemy says. You are destined for greatness and I believe in you. Go be fruitful in whatever your hands touch, and may it multiply as the Father gives you strength and favor. You are a champion! You are a winner. I love you very much, but God loves you more. Go and write your visions. Father says make it plain, because soon, you are going to run with it and the season is here that it will bless many. (Habakkuk 2:2)

Lovingly,
Armetria

About the Author

Armetria M. Charles is an exciting motivator, Christian life empowerment coach, and inspiring author whose passion is encouraging others to achieve their God-given destiny and equipping us to speak in our God-given authority. Her dream is to enlighten and equip the masses to own their personal greatness. Through motivational speaking and empowerment coaching, Armetria provides individuals with the practical tools and resources to make significant changes in their life.

Armetria feels her focus is "not to deal with symptoms, but rather to uproot issues and destroy destructive yokes."

In 2009, Armetria M. Charles founded the non-profit organization Tamar Speaks™ to expand her message of personal and spiritual development for survivors of sexual abuse or rejection, and to ensure the lives she encounters are forever changed through her messages of God's love.

Armetria has journeyed from pain to purpose. She is a faithful wife and devoted mother of five noble sons.

If you're interested in receiving one-on-one coaching with Mrs. Charles, please visit www.armetriamcharles.com.

For those interested in group coaching with Mrs. Charles, please visit www.mylifecompass.com/armetria.

Armetria is a firm believer in building the Virtuous Business Woman

www.virtuousaromas.com

To book Armetria M. Charles for your next speaking engagement, contact Phenomenal Events at 877-231-5287.

CPSIA information can be obtained at www.ICGtesting.com
229947LV00003B/5/P